IN SEARCH OF ALTERNATIVES
TRIBAL WOMEN IN DESERT SCENARIO

In Search of Alternatives
Tribal Women in Desert Scenario

SAMIRA DASGUPTA

GYAN

GYAN PUBLISHING HOUSE

NEW DELHI-110 002

In Search of Alternatives : Tribal Women in Desert Scenario
(Anthropology, Sociology, Women's Studies)

ISBN : 81-212-0497-6

Published 1995 in india by
Gyan Publishing House
5 Ansari Road
New Delhi 110 002

Printed at Tarun Offset Press, Delhi-110 053

In memory of my Father-in-law
and maternal Father-in-law,
Late Naresh Chandra Sarkar
and Late Mrinmoy Ghosh

Preface

The present book deals with the tribal women who work in construction site as unskilled labourers beside their occupation of cultivation. The study is done among the Bhil women of Rajasthan who are attached with this type of work. The author became so interested to study them when she had got an opportunity to go through the studies on these women who do such a hard work daily from dawn to dusk. Several questions came to her mind that how these women do such hard work, why they have become attached with it what is their position at the work site and also in their family, village and society. Being provoked with the limited studies on this type of women, the author has dicided to study the women construction labourers.

The study is done through the following chapters namely Chapter I Introduction which introduces the study to the readers. Chapter II Working venue and workers deals with the location of the construction sites where the women work. It also describes the work structure from proprietor to the women labourers to see how they are interlinked with each other. Chapter III The women at work deals with the women at their work site that is in the constrcution site. It describes when, how and from where these women became attached with the construction work? What are the reasons for their attachment with the construction work. It states what are the jobs they have to do, their wages, payment, working hours, behaviour and attitude of the contractors, their supervisors, towards them and their position in the construction site. Chapter IV Women in the home deals with the workers at their home. What are the jobs they have to do, whether any priviledge is given to them or not, whether they are regarded as very important persons in their home or not. How their earnings are spent. Chapter V Opinion Survey gives an idea about these women through various opinions by various persons such as the contractor, supervisor, mason, labourers, and villagers etc. Opinion is also collected from the women workers about how their villagers, employers treat them, what they think about these women. It ultimately gives an idea of status of women. In the Chapter VI of conclusion, basing on this study conclusion is drawn. In appendix some cases are described.

In connection with the work, the author is highly indebted to the Director of Anthropological Survey of India for providing the author various opportunities. The author expresses her sincere gratitude to Dr. B.B. Goswami, the then Deputy Director of Anthropological Survey of India, Western Region for his supervision and inspiration in the work. She is very much grateful to Prof. P.K. Bhowmick of Department of Anthropology, Calcutta University, Shri B.N. Banerjee, Reader, Department of Anthropology, Calcutta University for their valuable suggestions. The author also remembers the inspirations, suggestions she got during her work from Shri Bageshwar Singh, Anthropologist (Retd.) and Smt. Asha Datta, the then Research Associate, Psychology, Anthropological Survey of India. She is also grateful to them. The author shows her greatfulness to all the informants, contractors and the other officials, except their co-operation it would not be possible for her to complete the work.

Lastly she gives her special thanks to her husband Dr. Amitabha Sarkar, Anthropologist, Anthropological Survey of India, for his co-operation, inspiration and suggestions in each and every step of work. She is thankful to all her well wishers and typist Kumari Shanta Bala, Jagdalpur for their help and co-operation on various stages of this work.

Contents

	Preface	*vii*
1	Introduction	1
2	Working Venue and Workers	14
3	Women at Work	29
4	Women in the Home	73
5	Opinion Survey	83
6	Position of Bhil Women in their Society	92
7	Conclusion	96
	Appendix-I	*103*
	Appendix-II	
	Bibliography	*134*
	Index	*137*

1

Introduction

There are several studies in anthropology and sociology on working women, some are on women in relation to the changing economic scene, some on motivation which leads women to work; a few deals with role conflict. Many authors have tried to examine the effects of employment on a woman's life and upbringing of children. The main focus of these studies, as it seems, is on the status of women. The Indian council of Social Research are studying the status of women in the country. There are other researches as well who studied Indian Women. Hate (1946, 1948) discussed chief motivation for working and about dual role of women. Kapur (1960) showed attitudes of educated working Hindu women (quoted by Kala Rani, 1976); Sengupta (1960) studied women employed in mines, factories, plantation, agriculture, service, business and other professions from unskilled menial labour to educated women. Kapur (1970) worked on marriage and working women; she dealt with marital adjustment problems for married, educated and working Hindu women. Bhatty (1971) worked on the problems faced by the educated working women ; Singh (1972) concluded that the motivation to employment is closely related to role conflict. Patil (1972) wrote on women executives and concluded that woman's successful and extraordinary career brings danger in marital life. Rani (1976) showed that it was difficult for working women to carry on two roles together; and she joins hand with Kapur (1970) that main cause of maladjustment and conflict is refusal of husband to share household work and their hostility to their wives' employments.

Beside these studies Dasgupta (1978) worked on industrialization and published a paper where he discussed about the tribal women labourers. Similarly, Banerjee (1978) gave some information, through his paper on 'Tribal Women in a coal field area'.

Though women in the lower strata of society on economic ladder have been working keeping shoulder to shoulder with men from many days as daily wage earners in factories, mines, at construction sites, as maid servants, yet there are very few studies on these working women.

Being provoked with the limited studies on such category of working women, interest being taken to study those women of lower strata of economic as well as in the social ladder.

According to 1971 census among 31 million working women in India 29 million (94%) are engaged in the unorganized sector (Women construction workers; G.P. Sinha, S.N. Ranade, ICSSR). Among them 81.4% are engaged in agricultural sector. The works in non-agricultural sector are of various types, namely live stock keeping, mining and quarrying, manufacturing, construction, trade, commerce and transport.

Women in construction work interested the author. Generally these women work as casual labourer and are involved in hard arduous physical labour to earn the minimum wages. In India 0.2 million women and same number of men are engaged in construction work (Census of India, 1971).

In Rajasthan 0.6% of female workers are engaged in construction work while the percentage of males in the construction work is 0.4% only (Census of India, 1971).

There are number of studies on women construction workers. The first is of Sinha (1975) whose locale is in and around Patna and other is by Ranade (1975) who worked in Delhi.

Sinha in his study of Bihar discussed employment, recruitment, wages, working conditions, socio-demographic characteristics of the respondents and the economic status.

According to Ranade the unskilled labourers are mainly (86%) of the rural poor persons from Rajasthan. He discussed age of respondent, age at which she was first employed, nature and duration of employment, total number of jobs taken, wages, economic condition and socio-demographic characteristics.

The two studies are exploratory and exhaustive. The works done on socio-demographic characteristics of women in the industry, system of recruitment, general service conditions, types of work, wages, health, living and welfare activities and economy to identify and assess the specific nature of their problems.

Sengupta (1980) gave a picture of women construction labourers. She called these women as women of the dust. She appealed that much more care must be given to their living and working conditions than is being done at present.

Guha Thakurta (1980) worked in Tripura among the contract labourers in construction industry. His study covered both skilled and unskilled labourers of both the sexes.

Prasad (1988) dealt with the economic and physical exploitation of the tribal woman labourers.

Saran and Sandhwar (1990) in their book identified and tried to understand the problems of the women who work as unskilled labourers in brick kiln, quarries and mines in Bihar and West Bengal.

The present study is done at Udaipur district of Rajasthan among the women labourers belonging to the tribal groups engaged as unskilled labourers in construction work. Proposed site for work is selected in and around Udaipur, which is developing rapidly with a lot of construction work. Udaipur is selected for the study because there are many construction sites, where maximum number of labourers come from the tribal communities.

In this study the first duty was to select a suitable site. Here suitable site means a big construction site consisted of atleast 120-150 informants of predecided type. For this study longer stay with them is helpful to establish a good rapport. Longer stay could enable to collect some important observational data on interpersonal relationship and also the data collected through various other anthropological techniques can be checked. At Udaipur city itself, majority of those work sites were of small magnitude and of private building construction which includes two to at the most ten women. In this situation with the help of State Labour Officer, a construction site in the industrial area of Udaipur was selected for the work. It was a construction site of a factory (of production of synthetic yarn) whose proposed name was Reliance Chemotex Textile Industries. It was private construction work where there were 60 to 70 women labourers of whom 63 are the tribal belong to the Bhil community.

By this time a schedule is prepared and to test its suitability, six tribal women construction labourers were interviewed in the city proper. After that necessary corrections are made in the schedule and made it ready for data collection from the women construction labourers.

Data were collected from 1979 to 1980 by close observation and interview technique. After completion of data collection at Reliance Chemotex construction site, data were collected from the Bhil women labourers at four other construction sites at Udaipur city which are small projects in comparison to the site of Reliance Chemotex mills where there are only about 10 workers constructing small private residential houses.

Lastly the big construction site in the mining area at Udaipur; that is, at Zawar Mines (mines of Hindustan Zinc Limited) was selected as the locale of the study. In Zawar Mines area there was the construction of the residential quarters for the Mines employees. The construction work was large project under three private contractors. In this construction site also the tribal women belong to the Bhil community who worked there as labourers.

The Zawar Mines area was selected to substantiate the data and also to locate if there is any difference between the women workers in two defferent situations, that is; one very close to city and the other in the mining area which is isolated and is far away from the city.

The anthropological tools and techniques namely interview and observation with case study are used for data collection.

The author in this work tried to study the way of life of the tribal women who work as construction labourers. She has collected data on their work, causes of motivation towards this type of job, problems faced by them in the construction site, facilities they are given by the employers, and also tried to study the role they play and status they enjoy in the construction site and also in their society. Beside these, a brief ethnography was also collected on the Bhils to understand their socio-economic life. Main emphasis is given to see the emergent way of life of the tribal women labourers who come to the construction site as unskilled wage earners.

The study has mainly two divisions :

(a) The women workers in the construction site—why, when and how they become construction labourer and also where (in which place—far or near) they come to work. Moreover, their work, wage, their position in the construction site and relationship with others also have been studied.

(b) These women at their home—this part dealt with their family, kins and villagers. Their attitude towards these women and vis-a-vis. Their position in their families and villages also have been studied.

From each and every site only the tribal women were the main focus of the study. All of them are Bhil. Altogether 120 Bhil women construction labourers have been included in the study. Separate case for each are also noted.

Here in the following lines a brief note on the Bhils is mentioned.

The Bhils are the second largest tribe of India and are one of the major tribes of Rajasthan. According to 1981 census they are 7,367,973 distributed in the states of Gujarat, Madhya Pradesh, Maharashtra and Rajasthan. They are also found sporadically distributed in Andhra Pradesh and Mysore. A few of them are seen at Tripura who have migrated and settled there as teagarden labourers. In Rajasthan they are mainly concentrated in southern Rajasthan and are 1840,966 (1981 census) in number.

The word Bhil, probably is derived from the Dravidian word Vil, meaning bow or bow man. They speak Bhilli. Some of them speak Vaghri and many of the Bhils can understand Hindi.

The Bhils have well built body with medium to short stature, dark to light brown complexion. They have mesocephalic head, round to oblong face, mesorrhine to platyrrhine nose often depressed at the root; straight or somewhat retreating forehead; well develop supra-orbital ridge, broad massive jaws, brown to dark brown eyes.

Regarding their origin there are several beliefs. In the early sanskrit literature it is mentioned that they belong to the Pulinda or Nishada race. Some of them believe that they have originated from a strange woman courted by the God Mahadeva. Some say that they are the descendants of Ekalavya; a great archer in Mahabharat.

The Bhil generally live in hilly and forest regions. Their traditional home covers the Aravalli, Vindya and Sutpura hills.

The literacy level of the Bhils as a whole in Rajasthan is very low and only 6.60%. The male and female literacy rates are 12.26% and 0.82% respectively.

The Bhils are a patrilineal tribe. Their families are mainly of nuclear type. The Bhil families staying in a hamlet or *phala* represent a common clan. They observe *phala* exogamy as a rule of marriage.

The Bhils are an endogamous tribe. Their social organization is characterised by the presence of diverse social groups recognized on the basis of kinship, territory, culture contact and religious tenants.

When the grouping is made on the basis of kinship, the Bhils are divided into two groups the *haga* and the *hagwadia*. The *haga* means the group consisted of blood related Kins and the *hagwadia* are the Kins related through the marriage bondage. Each of these two groups has several exogamous totemistic clans.

Territorially and socially the Bhils are divided into palia Bhils and Kalia Bhils. Larger territorial grouping is known as *Pal*. A *Pal* is consisted of a few *phalas*. *Pal* endogamy as a rule of marriage is not forbidden as it is consisted of several clans. The *Pali* Bhils are regarded as pure and of unmixed descent and the *Kalia* are treated by them as a group with lower social status due to their mixing with others. The *Palia* Bhils are called as *ujle* (pure or clean) and the Kalia as *mele* (impure or unclean) group. But the Kalia Bhils demand that they are the *ujle* Bhils as they are advanced by mixing with outside culture.

Religiously the Bhils are devided into two halves the Bhagats and non-Bhagats. As an influence of Hinduism some of the Bhils have gone through religious reformation and there was the rise in number of the devotees of the Bhagat faith. The Bhagats in general do not like to have any commensal and connubial relationship with the non-Bhagats.

In Rajasthan beyond these groupings the Bhils introduce themselves to the outsiders by several other endogamous groupings such as Gametia Bhil, Katara Bhil, Bhil Mama etc. The Gametia Bhils claim that they are the original settelers in Rajasthan and are descended from the Bhil rulers. The term Gametia denotes the head of the Bhil village. They are concentrated in the northern and the western Udaipur and.in some areas of the Sirohi district. They speak Mewari. The Gametia Bhils are divided into a number of exogamous, totemistic clans (*ataks*) such a Kharari, Eri, Dongri etc. They observe *phala* exogamy. Each of the clans has separate deities.

Katara Bhils are distributed in Dhariavad, Ashpur, and Ghatol tehsils of Udaipur which were previously known as Katara. They are also distributed in Dungarpur and Banswara districts of Rajasthan. They speak Vaghri. They have approximately eighty four totemic clans (*ataks*).

Mama Bhils also speak Vaghri and are distributed in the Kushalgarh area of Rajasthan. They have no objection to make marital relationship with the Lengulia Bhils of Jhabua district of Madhya Pradesh.

For the present study social groups separately are not taken under consideration.

It is already mentioned that they mostly live in nuclear families. After marriage a son gets separated from his family of orientation and builds a separate hut where he begins to stay with his wife and children. A separate piece of land is allotted to him for the maintenance of the family by his father.

In a family, husband is the supreme authority. Descent is patrilineal. During divorce, the children are left with their father. The property is divided among the sons equally but succession is by the eldest son. The Bhil kinship system is of classificatory type.

Among the Bhils, pre-matal ritual is performed in the ninth month of pregnancy. It is known as *Kholo bherno.* A protective thread (*dore*) is given to the pregnant woman by a *bhagat* to wear. Delivery takes place at home assisted by a mid wife. The mid wife cuts the umbilical cord with a bamboo chip and buries that in a pit outside the house. They have a belief that in case of a female issue delivery takes place exactly after nine months and in case of a male issue it borns after nine months and some days. After delivery pollution period for the mother and the child starts and continues upto five days till they get purified through purificatory ceremony and lastly by a social feast. The tonsure (*mundan*) is performed for a child at its age of one year and a quarter or later.

The Bhils practice territorial and clan exogamy as their marriage rules. They do not like to arrange marriage of their children during rainy season (July to October). Cousin marriage is not allowed among them. They are monogamous but polygyny is also permitted. A Bhil with more than a wife gets a higher social and economic status in their society. Marriage by purchase, exchange, service intrusion and elopement are allowed. Natra or widow marriage is also permitted and in case of a widow junior levirate is encouraged most. Similarly sororate is also allowed. They have a custom of payment of bride price or *dapa*. Bride price is paid both in cash and kind. Prepuberty marriage followed by *gaona* existed in their custom as at that time child marriage was prevalent. Now they mostly practice adult marriage.

After finalization of marriage, both the parties prepare two small threads from the bark of a tree and tie nine knots after making it yellow by rubbing it with turmeric. The two parties exchange the threads with each other. From nine days before marriage everyday one knot is un-tied.

There are six phases of marriage, each is called as Vana or Vano, each of those are conducted separately at the bride's and bridegroom's house. In *piti*, a mixture of turmeric and flour is applied to the bride and bridegroom in their respective houses. In second phase they pay respect to the streets, lanes and sacred places of the village. In the third phase they show respect to the deity named Bharma who is responsible to protect them from all the evil spirits. In the fourth phase they worship their ancestral deities. The fifth phase is so interesting where they worship a pipal tree by offering a small cot to it. The small cot is offered to the tree so that the couple may always have a bed to rest on. In sixth phase they pay homage to the marrige deity.

Marriage takes place at the bride's house. Phera or seven rounds to the sacred thread by the bride and the bridegroom is one of the very important part of marriage. The nuptial ceremony is observed a day after marriage following the bidai (a ritual of sending daughter to her in-law's house). Lac bangles and silver anklets are regarded as marriage symbols for a married woman.

Divorce is permitted for both the sexes. In case of a man wants to divorce his wife, informs the panchayat and infront of the panchayat, he ties five rupees at the corner of his wife's sari and tears off a little piece of his turban and gives it to the wife as a symbol of breaking the relationship. When a woman wants to divorce her husband, her parents or would be husband has to return back the bride price to the man which his family paid during his marriage with the woman.

The Bhils cremate their dead but in case of a *bhagat*, he is burried. On the third day they get purified by shaving, cleaning and taking the purificatory bath. This is known as *Kol padsa mandal*. After performance of this ritual they are allowed to go to field or to join the work. But traditionally the pollution period lasts for twelve days when a man dies and eleven days in a woman's death. This is followed by *padgi rasam* ceremony where they have to give a dinner to the kins and relatives and get completely purified. From the day till one year they offer food and drink twice a day to the dead person. They install a menhir or a memorial stone which is called *gatha*. This is erected in a grove regarded as the dwelling place of the ancestors. In each and every village there is a place where menhirs are erected with stand for the Bhils ancestors of the village.

In the uni-ethnic villages the Bhil have their own panchayat of social control. The panchayat is constituted by the village elders. Most issues are referred to the village headman who is known as Gameti or Mukhiya or Patel. In larger multi *phala* villages there are *phala gametis* to sort out intra-*phala* and inter *phala* disputes. In case of inter-*phala* dispute, the case is referred to the *gameti* of the dominant *phala*. They are primarily the cultivators. They practise settled cultivation. They cultivate maize, millet, wheat, rice, pulses, barley etc. Their economy is supplemented by domestication of animals, collection of various types of edible roots, fruits, tubers, honey etc. from jungle, and also by hunting and fishing. At present hunting became an occasional phenomena. On the other hand many of them became wage earners. They mainly get involved as wage earners in agricultural sectors, or in construction sites as unskilled wage earners. There are a very few persons do some white collar jobs.

They believe that the Bhagwan (God) is the supreme diety. They worship all the natural objects such as mountain, river, trees, forest, sun, moon as the abode of benevolant spirit. They pay respect to pipal, and mango trees. They also worship agricultural tools, implements, manure etc. Their ancestores are regarded as deities and worshipped to time to time. They follow both traditional tribal and Hindu religion. Holi is an important festival to them. They also celebrate Dussehra and Diwali. The Hindu deities namely Ambaji, and Srinathji are very important to them. Impact of these

Hindu deities in their socio-cultural domain clearly reflex Bose's idea of Hindu method of tribal absorption (1941). They always are afraid of some ghosts and spirits. They make offerings of small clay horses, jars etc. to the ghosts and spirit to appease them. They have their own priest and medicineman.

The Bhils have been involved in a number of movements such as Bhakti movement into the Bhil area. The Bhakti movement divided them into Bhagat and non Bhagat. The second type of movement is related to land and forest was particularly found in the Dhulia district of Maharashtra in mid 1970. The third movement was of political nature where in 1940, the Bhil raised a demand for the creation of a separate state but it was never well articulated.

2

Working Venue and Workers

It is already mentioned that the study has been conducted in Udaipur district of Rajasthan. The work is done in and around its walled city that is in Udaipur city which is walled by Aravalli ranges and situated in its valley. All the construction sites are situated in Girwa tehsil of Udaipur district.

Among the two big construction sites, the first one; that is; Reliance Chemotex Textile Industries is situated in the east cross part of Udaipur district and which is the south-east portion of Girwa tehsil, in the industrial area, approximately 10 kms. far from the city and close to the old city station. The venue is surrounded by village Kanpur in east, village Madri in west, old city station that is Rana Pratap Nagar in north and Sarda tehsil in south. It is the construction site for a textile mill covering an area of about 10 acres. Here in this construction site proposal is there to build the mill consisted of the main building or the workshop and the administrative building. There is also a plan to build the staff quarters. At the time of study the construction work of the mill has already been started.

The second construction site is situated in the mining belt of Udaipur district, the Zawar Mines. It is the mines of Zinc. Zawar Mines are situated in the southern part of Girwa tehsil of Udaipur district which is about 50 kms. far from the Udaipur city. It is the site for the construction of 'A' type residential quarters for class IV staff of the mines. It is 4 kms. away in south from the administrative office, workshop blocks. The place is named by the mines' authority as Ashok Nagar. Ashok Nagar is surrounded by village Relan in east, mines office in west, Zawar railway station in north and village Padla in south. The construction work started in March 1979. It is a contract of one year for construction of 27 buildings undertaken by two contractors.

Except these two large construction sites the other four sites are selected in the city of Udaipur. All the construction sites are situated very close to each other and situated in the west of the city. All these are privately owned residential quarters under three contractors.

In a construction site everybody from the proprietor to labourer has definite work and responsibility to do. They all are linked or connected with each other through their work or responsibilities which leads to build a definite work structure. Therefore a construction work forms the network of relations connecting the workers amongst themselves.

These six construction sites are of various types such as to construct a mill, privately owned house and residential staff quarters. Their work structure is discussed below.

For construction of the mill of Reliance Chemotex Textile Industries as shown in Table 1 it is observed that there is a definite work structure from proprietor to labourer having definite responsibilities or works to perform and they are connected through the network of relationship by work with each other.

At Reliance Chemotex textile mills the proprietor called for a tender of Rs. 25 lakhs for construction of mill. A contract is agreed with a Jain contractor of Jaipur for construction of the building. There are several engineers, and officials along with the contractor who are directly appointed by the proprietor. The engineers are appointed by proprietor to make the plans for construction of mills. Mill's officials are to supervise the materials which are required by and supplied to the contractor and to keep the accounts on expenditure for construction. The contractor has the overall responsibility of the construction of the building of the mill.

Under each of the three heads; that is; the engineers, officials and the contractors, there are many other persons to work. Since the present study concerns workers with special emphasis to the women, the structure is traced from the contractor downward to casual labourers.

Under the contractor, there are two supervisors, one clerk- *cum*-accountant-*cum*-overseer, two peons and eleven petty contractors for various types of works.

The supervisors are appointed to supervise the work situation, to solve various types of problems and difficulties in work, to keep the workers busy with work during working hours. One of the supervisors has overall responsibility that is; to keep an eye in all sorts of works at the construction site, to keep knowledge about the quantity and quality of the materials supplied by the proprietor's officials, materials needed, problems at work, progress and regularities of work, needs and demands of labour.

The other supervisor only controls and supervises the labourers and their works. He keeps himself engaged in the contractor's another business of transport which is many times needed in construction site to bring the labourers from their villages and other similar types of works are done by him.

The clerk keeps accounts. All the money is spent through the contractor's hand. He only keeps the accounts.

Both the peons are appointed to do the works as ordered by the contractor, his supervisors and the clerks. One of the peon is appointed to carry water and supply it to all of the workers. He is Brahman by caste. The another peon's main work is to guard the materials.

The eleven petty contractors under the main contractor, got their contracts of various types of works namely digging, pile work, brick masonry, stone masonry, sheeting of the roof by asbestos, fabrication and erection work, wood work, finishing and white washing.

The supervisors have their subordinates to assist in their work. They are generally known as mates and submates. They carry out the orders of the supervisors. The mates and submates generally help the supervisors in their work of labour supervision. The supervisors have the power to select the mates and submates who are generally appointed from the group of labourers. The mates are regarded as the representatives from the side of labourers. Therefore, it is easy for the supervisor to control the groups of labourer through the mates and submates and on the other hand it is easy for the labourers to put their demands to the supervisor through the mates and submates. The mates and submates work as the bridge between supervisors and labourers. The supervisors also have an added responsibility to meet demands of the labourers time to time. The mates and submates bring the demands of the labourers to the supervisor(s). The supervisors sort out those and bring forth to the contractor.

The labourers are of all the three categories that is skilled, semi-skilled and unskilled. Only unskilled labourers are found of both the sexes, the other two categories of labourers that is skilled and semi-skilled labourers are only consisted of male members.

Under the contractor for digging there are labourers of both the sexes. The men dig the soil (three women are also expert in this work). Women mainly collect those soil and throw those at another place. Pile work is done by men, assisted by women.

Two contractors are appointed for the masonry work. One of them is for brick masonry and the other stone masonry. Under the contractor for brick masonry and stone masonry there are masons and labourers. Masons are men and the labourers are of both the sexes. Among the labourers some prepare the concrete mixture who are called as beldars and the others are as *coolie* or helpers. It is found that the contractors of both stone masonry and brick masonry appointed men as belder. Helpers, or the *coolie* are found of both the sexes.

Some of the portion of the roof is made by R.C.C. (by concreting) work but the rest portion is made by asbestos. A contractor is appointed for asbestos sheeting. He has only the male labourers.

The charge of fabrication and erection work is taken by another contractor who has only the male labourers. He has drillers, welders and labourers. All of them are male.

After that to prepare doors, windows, a contract is given to a carpenter who has all male labourers under him.

Electrical works are done by a contractor. He has some male workers under him.

The finishing work is under a contractor. He has only male labourers.

There is a Sunni contractor for sanitory fitting. He has some male labourers under him.

White washing and painting is similarly done by a separate contractor. He also has male labourers.

The proprietor is the Agarwal Jain of Jaipur. The contractor under him is also a Jain, a friend of the proprietor. The contractor has two supervisors. One is a Brahman originally from Madras directly appointed by the contractor. The other is the Rajput of Jaipur who is appointed through his uncle. The peons are directly recruited by the contractor. Both are originally from Udaipur of Rajasthan. One of them is Brahman and the other is Rajput by caste. The clerk is a Brahman of Udaipur recruited by the contractor.

Among the eleven petty contractors, the contractor of digging is a Banjara man under whom all the labourers are Banjara. This Banjara man is directly attached with the contractor since nine years, from the time of huge project at Dabok. The contractor for pile work and all his labourers belong to the Meghwal caste.

He is also directly connected with the contractor from the time of the work at Lake Palace hotel, Udaipur. The contractor for brick masonry is a Muslim of Sunni sect from Bihar. Under him the masons are either Muslim of Sunni sect of Bihar or are the Bhils of Udaipur. The contractor of stone masonry is a Jain of Ajmer. Under him there are Kumawat, Bhil and Rajput masons. The labourers belong

Table 1
Construction of Mill

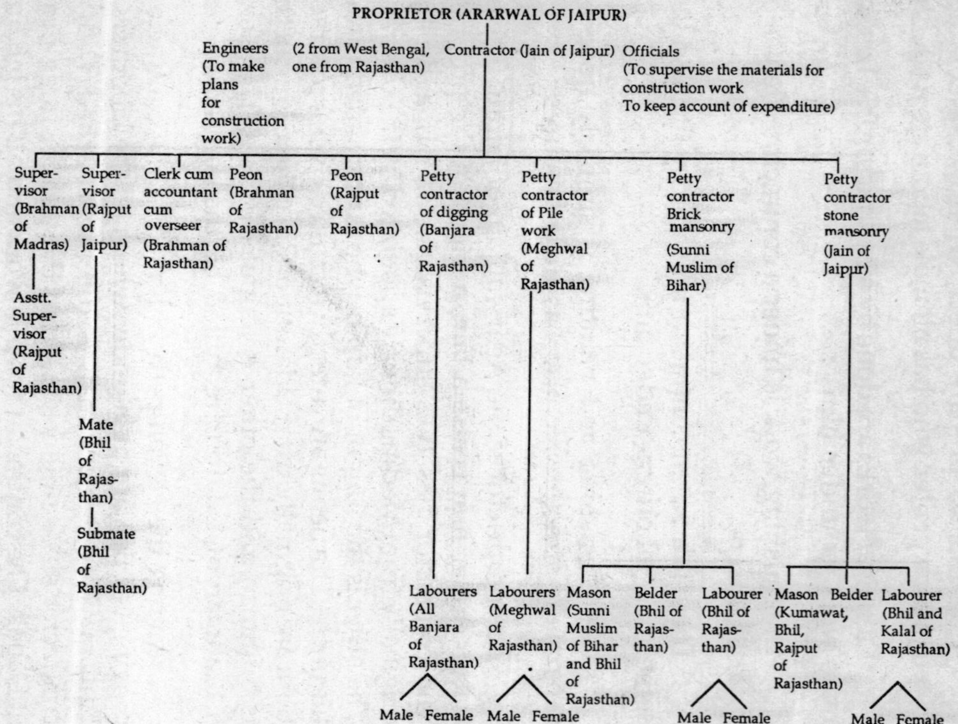

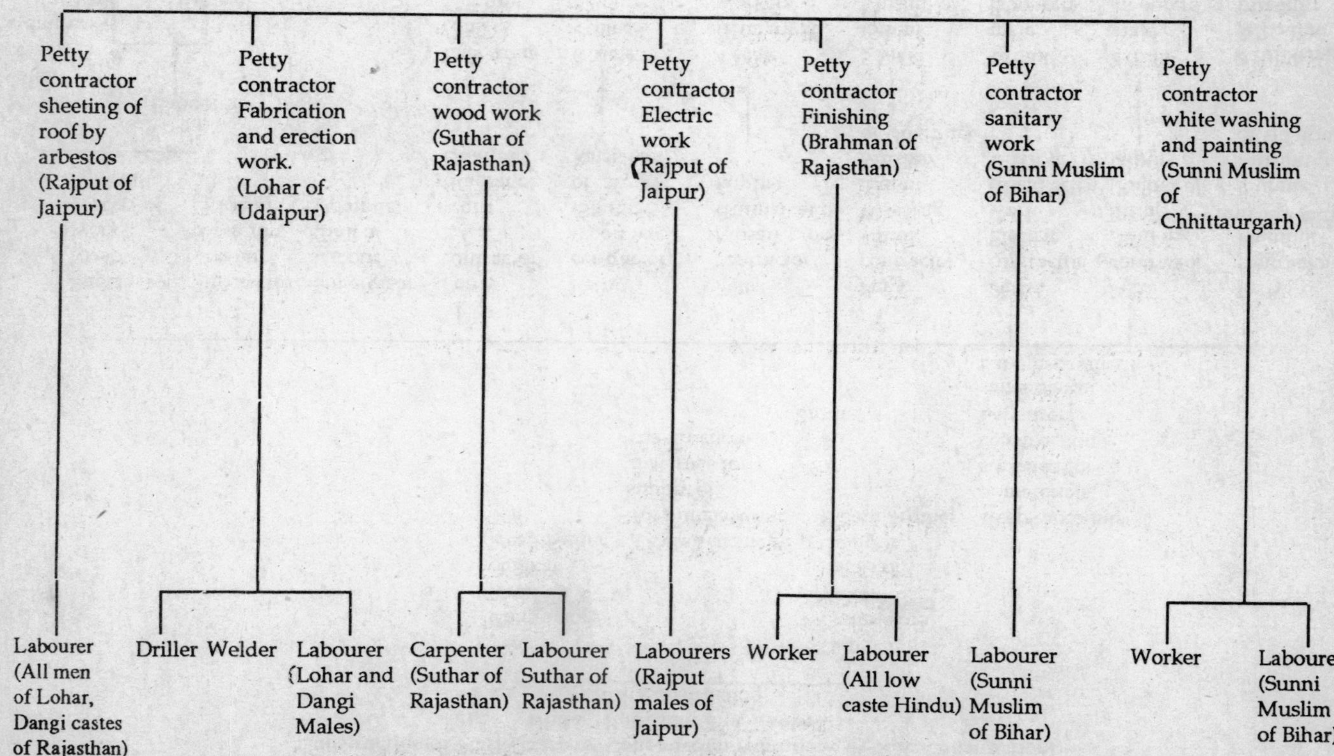
Petty contractor sheeting of roof by arbestos (Rajput of Jaipur)
Petty contractor Fabrication and erection work. (Lohar of Udaipur)
Petty contractor wood work (Suthar of Rajasthan)
Petty contractor Electric work (Rajput of Jaipur)
Petty contractor Finishing (Brahman of Rajasthan)
Petty contractor sanitary work (Sunni Muslim of Bihar)
Petty contractor white washing and painting (Sunni Muslim of Chhittaurgarh)
Labourer (All men of Lohar, Dangi castes of Rajasthan)
Driller
Welder
Labourer (Lohar and Dangi Males)
Carpenter (Suthar of Rajasthan)
Labourer Suthar of Rajasthan)
Labourers (Rajput males of Jaipur)
Worker
Labourer (All low caste Hindu)
Labourer (Sunni Muslim of Bihar)
Worker
Labourer (Sunni Muslim of Bihar)

Table 2

Construction of Staff Quarters (Construction work done by K.K. Construction)
Under Hindustan Zinc Limited

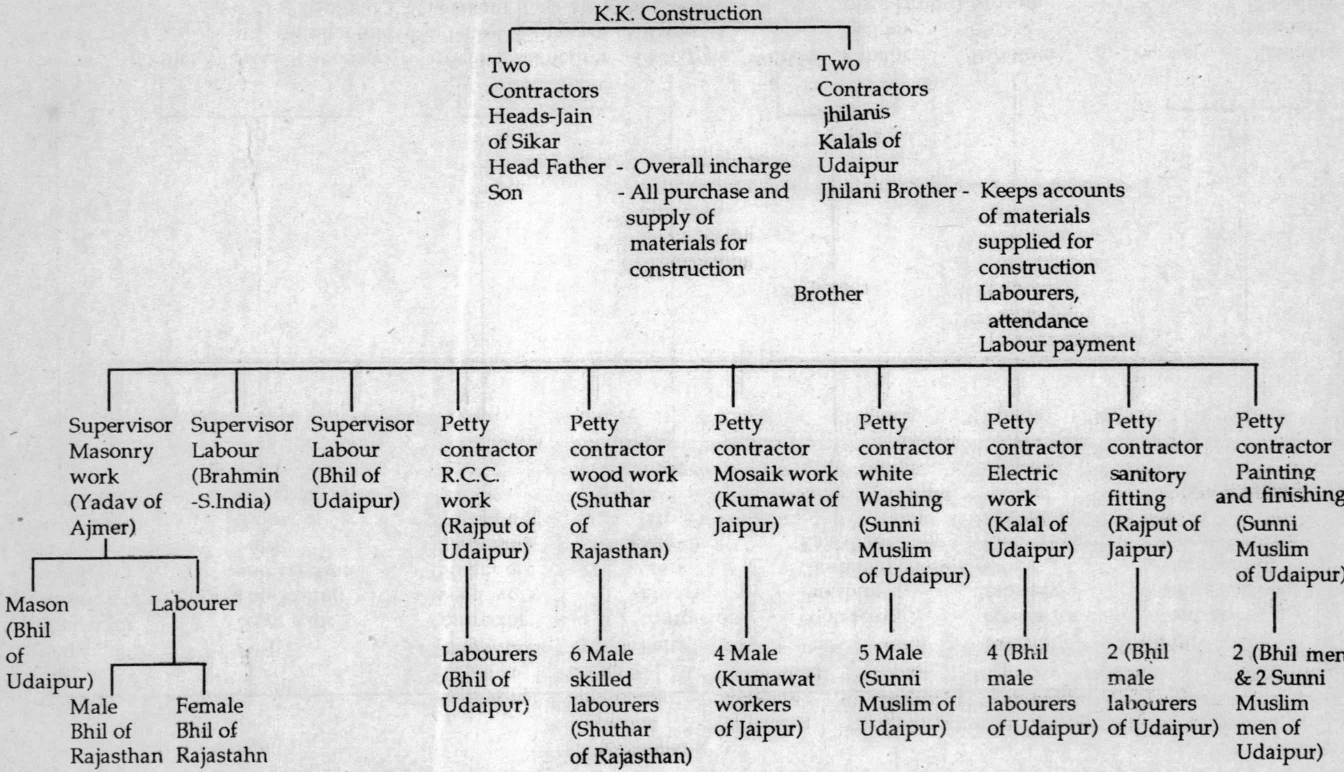

to the Kalal caste. Under the Rajput contractor of Jaipur for sheeting roof by asbestos, there are Lohar and Dangi labourers. Some Lohar and Dangi labourers are appointed under the Lohar contractor of Udaipur for fabrication and erection work. Similarly, there are Suthar labourers under a Suthar contractor who has taken the contract of wood work. The contractor of electrical work is a Rajput of Jaipur and all the workers under him are also Rajput of Jaipur. The contractor of finishing work is a Brahman, newly appointed directly in the construction work. The labourers appointed under him are from the caste Hindu who occupy the lower position in ritual hierarchy. Under Sunni Muslim petty contractor of Bihar for sanitory finishing there are labourers from Bihar and under the Muslim contractor of Chittorgarh for white washing and painting, there are labourers, some of whom are Muslim of Sunni sect and the Bhil of Udaipur.

The assistant supervisors, under the supervisor are Rajput and they have Bhil mates and submates.

At the Zawar Mines, the construction work is undertaken by two agencies (i) K.K. construction and (ii) Chowdhury construction.

The K.K. Construction (Table 2) is jointly owned by Hedas (father and son) and Jhilanis (two brothers). These four persons that is two parties jointly have taken the work of this construction site for construction of 27 buildings. Contract for each building are rupees one lakh and thirty thousand. The contract money is divided into two equal halves. Hedas are responsible to purchase the materials from market needed for construction of the buildings and Jhilanis are responsible for payment of all types of works attached with the construction work under K.K. construction.

Again these four persons have different responsibilities. Among the Hedas the father is the overall incharge and the son deals with all the purchase and supply of materials. Among the Jhilani brothers, one keeps the accounts of materials supplied for construction work and the other keeps accounts of attendance of the labourers. He looks after their needs, working condition and progress of work and is responsible for labour payment.

Under these contractors there are three supervisors. One of them is appointed for supervision of masonry work. The other two are labour supervisors. There are seven contractors under these contractors who have taken contracts for various construction works. Among them one is given the contract of reinforcement cement concrete (R.C.C.) work, one for wood work, one for sanitory fitting work, one for mosaic work, one for white washing, one for painting and finishing and one for electric work.

Under the supervisor for masonry work, there are masons. The masons and the labourers are directly connected with the contractor of masonry work but the labour supervisors supervise the masons' and the labourers' work. The labourers belong to both the sexes, whereas, the masons are only the males. Among the labourers it is observed that the women hold the larger number than the men. Generally the male labourers work as belders (who prepare the concrete mixture and also build temporary platforms), some of the men are appointed for digging and the rest (a very negligible number) work as *coolie* or helper. The women here work as *coolie*. They carry concrete mixture, bring water, do watering on newly constructed walls, clean floors etc.

The contractor of wood work has six skilled male labourers. The contractor for sanitory work has two male labourers, mosaic work is done by another contractor who has four male members. There are five men work under the

Table 3
Construction of Staff Quarters (Construction work done by Chowdhury Construction)
Under Hindustan Zinc Limited
Contractor—Chowdhury (Jain of Jaipur)

Supervisor Overall Incharge (Oriya Kayastha)	Supervisor Masonary work (Kumawat of Udaipur)	Supervisor Labourer (Kalal of Rajasthan)	Petty Contractor R.C.C. work (Kalal of Udaipur)	Petty Contractor Wood work (Suthar of Rajasthan)	Petty Contractor White washing (Sunni Muslim of Udaipur)	Petty Contractor Mosaik work (Kumawat of Jaipur)	Petty Contractor Painting and finishing (Sunni Muslim of of Udaipur)	Petty Contractor Electrical work (Kalal of Udaipur)	Petty Contractor Sanitary firring (Rajput of Jaipur)
		Labourers (Bhil of Udaipur)	Labourers (Bhil of Udaipur)	6 Male skilled labourers (Suthar of Rajasthan)	5 Male (Sunni Muslim of Udaipur)	4 Male (Kumawat workers of Jaipur)	2 (Bhil men and 2 Sunni Muslim men of Udaipur)	4 (Bhil male labourers of Udaipur	2 (Bhil male labourers of Udaipur)

All these men are the same who are also attached with the K.K. Construction.

contractor for white washing. Two persons are appointed by the contractor of finishing and the contractor for electrification has only four persons as his helpers.

Among the contractors the Hedas are Jain belong to the Sikar district of Rajasthan. The Jhilani brothers are Kalal by caste and are originally from Udaipur district. Among the supervisors the man for masonry work belongs to the Yadav caste who is directly appointed by Hedas from Ajmer. The another supervisor is a Brahman from South India, now settled at Rajasthan. The third supervisor belongs to the Bhil community of Rajasthan. All of them are appointed with the work by the contractor. The Brahman supervisor and the Bhil supervisor do the job of labour supervision.

The contractor for R.C.C. work belongs to the Rajput caste of Udaipur. All his labourers belong to the Bhil community and all of them are from Udaipur.

There are some Shuthar males work under the Shuthar contractor for wood work. They all belong to the Udaipur.

The sanitory works are done by a Rajput contractor. All the labourers work under him are Bhil men of Rajasthan.

A Kumawat contractor with all his Kumawat labourers are involved in mosaic work. They have come from Jaipur.

A Sunni Muslim contractor is responsible for white washing and he has all Sunni Muslim labourers. They all belong to Udaipur.

The contractor for painting and finishing is also a Sunni Muslim of Udaipur. He has some Sunni Muslim and some Bhil labourers.

Electrical work is done by a Kalal contractor. He himself works with two Bhil labourers.

All the unskilled labourers for masonry works are Bhil and in maximum cases they are the women who mainly work as *coolie* or helper of the masons by carrying concrete mixture etc.

Chowdhury construction (Table 3) is under a contractor whose title is Chowdhury. He has five supervisors. One among them is overall incharge, one is appointed for supervision of masonry work and the rest three are the labour supervisors.

Chowdhury construction has seven contractors for R.C.C. work, wood work, white washing, mosaic work, painting and finishing, electric work and sanitation. Leaving aside the contractor for R.C.C. work, the rest six contractors are the same persons who work under K.K. Construction.

Under the supervisor for masonry work, there are masons who are directly recruited by contractor Chowdhury. The supervisors are only responsible to supervise the progress of work. The mason are all men, only the unskilled labourers are found of both the sexes.

Chowdhury is the Jain of Jaipur. He also has got the contract of an amount equal to the K.K. construction from the Hindusthan Zinc Limited.

Among Chowdhury's supervisors the overall supervisor is an Oriya Kayastha, the supervisor for masonry work is Kumawat by caste, and among the others one is a South Indian Christian man, one is a Kalal and another is a Rajput man. The other contractors are the same persons appointed under Heda except the contractor for R.C.C. work who is a Kalal. The masons are all from the Kumawat caste, the wood workers are Suthar, mosaic workers are Kumawat, white washing, painting, finishing are done by the Bhils and Sunni Muslim.

Chowdhury recruited all the workers directly.

Except these construction sites investigation is done in another four construction sites which are under three contractors. Under the contractors there are masons, labourers (unskilled and skilled) and electricians. The unskilled labourers are women and some of them are Bhil, some are Muslims and Kalals. The contractors belong to the castes Rajput, Kalal, Kayastha.

From the above mentioned work structures it is observed that among the workers, women are only engaged in unskilled type of jobs. Here in the present study in all the construction sites the women are studied only from the brick masonry work and it is observed that 90% (approx.) of the total unskilled labourers are women. Among the rest 10% (approx.) men labourers, nearly 8% work as *beldar* (who prepare the concrete mixture and the temporary platform for the work. Rest 2% work as *coolie*. The women labourers not only work as unskilled labourer but at the sametime they constitute the majority of the labourers at the construction sites. They mostly belong to the Bhil community. At Reliance Chemotex construction site in total there are 57 tribal and 11 non-tribal women labourers. Among the 57 tribal women labourers 45 who are attached with brick masonry, are interviewed. 29 women of those 45 interviewed women come from the villages Kanpur, Rata Khet, Dharicha, Rampur and Baran of Girwa tehsil. All these villages except Baran are situated at a distance 20 kms. (approx.) from the construction site. Village Kanpur is the nearest village and situated within 2 kms. from the construction site. Maximum number of labourers come from villages Rata Khet, Rampur, and Dharicha villages which are 18-20 kms. (approx.) away from the construction site. Women labourers also come from other tehsils such as Nathdwara, Kherwara and Mavli of Udaipur district and also from some villages of Dungarpur district. All the villages of these tehsils are not less than 50 kms. far from the Reliance Chemotex construction site. Deval village of Dungarpur district is more than 70 kms. from the construction site. The rest 16 workers studied, 13 come from Bilak village of Kherwara tehsil, and 1 each from Total, Palwas Kalan and Deval village of Dungarpur district.

There are 70 women engaged in brick masonry at Zawar Mines. Among them 16 come form the villages Baran, Chanabda, Haropal, Rewatalai, etc. of Girwa tehsil of Udaipur which are within 25 kms. from the construction site. 50 informants come from Padla, Relan, Leboda, Palodora, Kherki, Dhankabara villages of Sarda tehsil. Among these 50 women, 19 women come in a group from the village Padla. Three women come from Bilak village of Kherwara tehsil, one from Deval of Dungarpur district.

Except these a few more women are studied who come to work in other four construction sites from the villages Nimaj Kheda, Ratanpura and Diwali which are within 3 kms. far from the construction site.

It has been observed that among the total 120 women construction labourers studied, maximum number of women labourers come to work from the villages of Girwa tehsil and Sarda tehsil of Udaipur district and they are 50 (41.66%) respectively. 16(13.33%) come from Kherwara tehsil. From Total village of Nathdwara 1(0.83%) person, from Palwas Kalan village of Mavli come to work. The rest 2(1.66%) come from Deval village of Dungarpur district.

This chapter mainly deals with the work site, work structure and the places from where the women construction workers come to work. It is seen that the contractor is connected with all the workers and petty contractors taken contracts from him sometimes directly and in some cases indirectly. He isdirectly connected with the supervisors and the petty contractors directly while he is indirectly related or connected with the masons, the other skilled, semi-skilled and unskilled labourers through the supervisors or the petty contractors who are directly related with those persons. Sometimes the supervisors are seen to be connected with labourers through the mates and submates.

In a construction site, from digging, pile work, brick masonry, stone masonry, wood work, fabrication work to finishing works are done step by step without performance of the previous step next step of work cannot be done. All these works are interlinked with each other to finish a work.

It is important to note that among all the workers the women are only engaged in unskilled type of jobs. Here in the present study only the women labourer of brick masonry are included. The women construction labourers of the studied construction site mainly come from the Girwa and Sarda tehsils of Udaipur district. A very few come from other tehsils such as Nathdwara, Mavli and Deval village of Dungarpur district.

3

Women at Work

Employment is the way to improve the economic status. It helps for the betterment of the level of food availability, nutrition and level of other basic and essential demands.

In India the number of working women is less. According to 1971 census (ICSSR, 1975) among 264 million women, the number of women worker is 34 million that is 13% (approx.) of the total number of women in Indian population. Among those 34 million workers there are 10 million cultivators and 16 million agricultural labourers. Out of 34 million working women less than 1 million are educated constituting about 2.9% (approx.) of the total mumber of working women.

Only 2.9% (approx.) of the total number of working women are educated. About 90% women workers are employed on jobs requiring unskilled or very little skilled labour. Less interest is taken to train the women workers. Due to acute poverty the working class families cannot provide for educational or vocational training for daughters. This working class only has planning (though it is very little) for their sons or heirs. This lack of education and any vocational training leads the working class women to join in the unskilled labour.

In this study the tribal women construction labourers are taken into account and those who have completed 12 years of age are included in the study. As per the 'The Plantation Labour Act No. 69 of 1951 no child who has completed his/her 12th year of age shall be required or allowed to work in any plantation'. But there are atleast 10 children noted in the Reliance Chemotex construction site who work with their mother. In this study they are not included. Only the women who have completed their 12 years of age are included in the study.

In Rajasthan, the women from the castes of lower strata in social hierarchy and specially the tribal women do the unskilled type of jobs which are physically most exhausting tasks of menial labour.

Women construction workers mainly belong to the age from 13 years to 38 years (approx). Between this age group the women can do more labour. So the contractors prefer to recruit women of 13 to 38 years of age and most of the studied construction labourer belong to this age group. There are a few women above this age group engaged at the construction work but they are appointed by the contractors due to their good health and efficiency in the work (see table 4).

Table 4
Age Group of Women Labourers

Age Group (in years) Approx.	*Udaipur*		*Zawar Mines*		*Total*	
	Total	*%*	*Total*	*%*	*Total*	*%*
13-18	11	22.00	24	34.28	35	29.17
19-23	16	32.00	27	38.57	43	35.83
24-28	4	8.00	14	20.00	18	15.00
29-33	7	14.00	2	2.86	9	7.5
34-38	6	12.00	2	2.86	8	6.66
39-43	2	4.00	1	1.43	3	2.5
44-48	2	4.00	-	-	2	1.67
49-53	2	4.00	-	-	2	1.67
54-58	-	-	-	-	-	-
59+	-	-	-	-	-	-
	50	100.00	70	100.00	120	100.00

Table 6
Age at which women join the construction site

Sl. No.	*Age group (Complete years)*	*Construction site*				*No.*	*%*
		Udaipur		*Zawar Mines*			
		No.	*%*	*No.*	*%*		
1.	Below 13 years of age	22	44	11	15.71	33	27.50
2.	13-18	12	24	34	48.58	46	38.34
3.	19-23	6	12	17	24.28	23	19.17
4.	24-28	6	12	6	8.57	12	10.00
5.	29-33	2	4	1	1.43	3	2.50
6.	34-38	1	2	-	-	1	0.83
7.	39-43	1	2	1	1.43	2	1.66
8.	44-48	-	-	-	-	-	-
9.	49-53	-	-	-	-	-	-
10.	54-58	-	-	-	-	-	-
11.	59+	-	-	-	-	-	-
Total		50	100	70	100.00	120	100.00

Table 5 (A)

Family Type of the Informant

Place	Type of family	Women											
		Unmarried		Married		Widow		Separated		Divorced		Total	%
Udaipur	Nuclear	9	18%	19	38%	-	-	2	4%	-	-	30	60
	Joint	7	14%	5	10%	-	-	1	2%	-	-	13	26
	Broken	-	-	-	-	1	2%	-	-	-	-	1	2
	Incomplete	-	-	4	8%	-	-	-	-	-	-	4	8
	Single membered domicile/Individual	-	-	-	-	2	4%	-	-	-	-	2	4
Zawar Mines	Nuclear	35	50%	1	1.42%-	-	-	1	1.42%	-	-	37	52.86
	Joint	22	31.42%	4	5.71%	-	-	5	7.14%	-	-	31	44.28
	Broken	1	1.42%	-	-	-	-	1	1.42%	-	-	2	2.86
	Incomplete	-	-	-	-	-	-	-	-	-	-	-	-
	Individual/Single membered domicile	-	-	-	-	-	-	-	-	-	-	-	-
Total (U+Z)	Nuclear	9+35=44	-	19+1=20	-	-	-	-	2+1=3	-	-	67	55.83
	Joint	7+22=29	-	5+4=9	-	-	-	-	1+5=6	-	-	44	36.67
	Broken	0+1=1	-	-	-	1+0=1	-	-	0+1=1	-	-	3	2.5
	Incomplete	-	-	4+0=4	-	-	-	-	-	-	-	4	3.33
	Single membered domicile/Individual	-	-	-	-	2+0=2	-	-	-	-	-	2	1.67
Total		16+58=74		28+5=33		3+7=10	-	-	-	-	-	120	100.00
		(32%)	(82.85%)	(56%)	(7.14%)	(6%)	(6%)		(14%)	-	-	-	-

Table 7

First coming in the construction site with the Person (generation-wise)

Sl. No.	*With whom the women came to join the work (person of)*	*Construction sites*				*No.*	*%*
		Udaipur		*Zawar Mines*			
		No.	*%*	*No.*	*%*		
1.	One generation above	24	48	12	17	36	30.00
2.	Same generation	25	50	52	74.28	77	64.17
3.	One generation below	-	-	2	2.85	2	1.66
4.	Alone	1	2	4	5.71	5	4.17

Table 8

Who brought the women to present construction work

Sl. No.	*With whom comes to work (Person of)*	*Construction sites*				*No.*	*%*
		Udaipur		*Zawar Mines*			
		No.	*%*	*No.*	*%*		
1.	One generation above	18	36	9	12.86	27	22.5
2.	Same generation	26	52	55	78.57	81	67.5
3.	One generation below	4	8	2	2.86	6	5.0
4.	Alone	2	4	4	5.71	6	5.0

Table 9

Attachment with the construction work through Kins/Non-Kins

Sl. No.	*Attachment through*	*Construction sites*				*No.*	*%*
		Udaipur		*Zawar Mines*			
		No.	*%*	*No.*	*%*		
1.	Consanguinal kin	18	36	47	67.14	65	54.17
2.	Affinal kin	11	22	2	2.86	13	10.83
3.	Non kin (village kin, friend)	20	40	17	24.29	37	30.83
4.	Alone	1	2	4	5.71	5	4.17

TABLE 5 (B)
MARITAL STATUS

Type of Labourer	UDAIPUR						ZAWAR MINES					
	Total	*Unm.*	*Marr.*	*Widow*	*Separated*	*Divorced*	*Total*	*Unm.*	*Marr.*	*Widow*	*Separated*	*Divorced*
	No.%	*No.%*	*No.%*	*No.%*	*No.%*	*No.%*	*No.%*	*No.%*	*No.%*	*No.%*	*No.%*	*No.%*
LOCAL	33 66.00 (of total 50)	7 21.21 (of total local lab. 33)	21 63.63	3 9.09	2 6.06	- -	30 42.85 (of total 70)	27 90.00 (of total 30)	- -	3 10.00	- -	- -
MIGRANT	17 34.00 (of total 50)	9 52.94 (of total migrant lab. 17)	7 41.17	- -	1 5.88	- -	40 57.14 (of total lab. 70)	31 77.5 (of total migrant lab. 40)	5 12.5	- -	4 10.00	- -
TOTAL	50	16 32.00 (of total 50)	28 56.00	3 6.00	3 6.00	- -	70 -	58 82.85 (of total 70)	5 7.14	- -	7 10.00	- -

TOTAL					
Total	Unm.	Marr.	Widow	Separated	Divorced
No.%	No.%	No.%	No.%	No.%	No.%
63 52.5	34 53.97	21 33.33	3 4.77	5 7.93	- -
57 47.5 (of total (120 lab)	40 70.18 (of total migrant lab 57)	12 21.05	- -	5 8.77	
120	74 61.67	33 27.5	3 2.5	5 8.33	

Table 10

Women coming with Kins/Non Kins

Sl. No.	*Coming with*	*Construction site*				*No.*	*%*
		Udaipur		*Zawar Mines*			
		No.	*%*	*No.*	*%*		
1.	Consanguinal Kin	16	32	42	60.00	58	48.33
2.	Affinal Kin	14	28	3	4.29	17	14.17
3.	Non Kin	18	36	21	30.00	39	32.5
4.	Alone	2	4	4	5.71	6	5.0

Here in the present study, 50 women are studied from Udaipur city, 45 work at the Reliance Chemotex Textile Industries and other 5 work at other construction sites in Udaipur city proper. In all these sites there are also children who are not included in the study. Only women of age from 13 years (approx.) upto 59+ are studied. Main working hand ranges between 13-38 years (approx.).

In the Zawar Mines 70 women are studied who belong to the age between 13 years to 43 years (approx.). Majority of the women are from the age group 13 years to 28 years (See in Table 4).

Table 5(a) describes the family of individual women workers. It is observed from the table that in all the sites majority of the women come from the nuclear families consisting of parents and unmarried children, sometimes with a dependent. In Udaipur city and in its industrial area it is 30(60%); and in case of Zawar Mines it is 37(52.86%). In total 120 studied women 67(55.83%) belong to the nuclear families.

Table 5(b) describes the marital status of the women construction labourers. At Udaipur there are 16(32%) unmarried, 28(56%) married, 3(6%) widow, 3(6%) separated women. Similarly at the Zawar Mines out of 70 women, 58(82.85%) are unmarried, 5(7.14%) are married, 7(10%) are separated. In a total 120 studied women, 74(61.66%) that is majority of the women are unmarried. There are 33(27.5%) married, 10(8.33%) separated women and 3(2.5%) widows. But it is very interestingly noted that in case of Udaipur, the number of married women labourers is more than the number of unmarried women while at the Zawar Mines the number of unmarried women is maximum and the married women are in a negligible number.

At the studied construction sites in Udaipur as per Table 5(b) it is found that among 50 labourers 33(66%) come in groups everyday early in the morning to the site to work from the local villages and after finishing the day's work they return home in the evening. Among those 33 local labourers, 21(63.63%) are married, 7(21.21%) are unmarried 3(9.09%) widow and 2(6.06%) are separated. Rest 17(34%) women are the migrant labourers who come to work from distant places from where it is not possible to come everyday. Those places are not less than 40 kms. away from the construction sites. There is no convence to cover such a distance. Moreover their villages are situated in the hills where only they can travel on foot. In such a condition those women temporarily migrate to the place of their work from their own villages and stay at the construction site for a period till they are attached with the construction site. Due to this reason, they are called here as migrant labourers. After completion of the work, they go back to their own village, stay there for a time till another suitable work comes. Among the 17 migrant labourers in Udaipur, there are 9(52.94%) unmarried, 7(41.17%) married and only 2(5.88%) separated women.

At Zawar Mines 30(42.85%) of the total 70 labourers are local labourers. Among them 27(90%) are unmarried, and 3(10%) are widow. No married woman is found to work from the local villages. Where as among 40(57.14%) migrant labourers, 31(77.5%) are unmarried, 5(12.5%) are married and 4(10%) are separated.

It is found from the above discussion that majority of the women construction labourers belong to the nuclear families. Among total 120 studied women, majority of them are unmarried. But interestingly it is also noted that the married women at the Reliance Chemotex site are more than the unmarried women come to work at the construction sites and they mostly come from the neighbouring village.

Another interesting point to mention is that the number of the local women labourers in Udaipur is greater than that of the Zawar Mines and in case of the Zawar Mines there is not a single married woman in such a group while at the Udaipur most of those women are married.

The migrant labourers at the Zawar Mines are more in comparison to the construction sites at the Udaipur. In the construction site at the Zawar Mines among the migrant labourers the number of unmarried labourers is more than the married women. Similarly in Udaipur also the total number of migrant, unmarried women labourers is more than the married women.

In all the studied cases it is observed that the unmarried women come to work at the construction site both as the local and the migrant labourers. In Udaipur the unmarried women are also accompanied by the married women who also work in the construction site and incidentally they are more in number. In the Zawar Mines, among the local labourers no married woman is noticed who come to work. Among the migrant labourers in all the sites the number of the married woman is very few and those who come to work, mostly come with their husband.

According to the persons of the villages situated close to Zawar Mines, they do not like to send their wives and married women of a family to work in the construction site. They believe that as it is an industrial area, people from various places and with various cultures come to work. Many males of them come alone leaving their families in their own places. Therefore, they may feel boaring or have a feeling of loneliness and a monotonous life inspite of earning a lucrative amount. To get rid of such a condition they may spend their money on drinks and for women and these are very common in this area. As they have money, they can easily attract the people who are in need of money and in this way the tribal women become attracted to them very easily and many times they are exploited sexually by those outsiders. Among the Bhils it is very shameful event to a husband and his family if his wife is sexually exploited or has some extra marital relationship with other. So they do not like to send their married women to work in the construction site. The unmarried women get more freedom till their marriage. So they are less hesitant to send their unmarried girls to work in the construction site.

In the Udaipur the situation differs. It is previously mentioned that the married women also accompany the unmarried women and they are more in number. Their family members and villagers also informed that they also do not want happily to send their married women to work in the construction site but due to economic pressure they are forced to send those to work in the construction site. According to them they send their women both married and unmarried to work in the construction site under the guardianship of a reliable, dependent person who keeps control over the whole group. Nobody can ignore or disobey him or her. The person keeps his or her strict eyes over all of the women under his or her control throughout the day. So it is not easy for a woman to do some mistake. Even then if anybody does some mistake she is warned and it is reported to her family. But they never allow their women to work outside as migrant labourers.

The women to work as migrant labourers are very few in number. They always come to work either with their husband or brother or son and daughter. They never allow their married women to come to work as migrant labourer alone without any family member. The cases of the separated women are completely different. They are comparatively free from many social bindings, many times they come to work as migrant labourers alone or along with their friends in a group.

Rajasthan is a very dry place where people are unable to produce enough for their consumption throughout the year. In such a condition they are forced to join other jobs including construction labour to earn their livelihood. Generally they do not prefer to send their women to work in the construction sites but their economic need forces them to send those for some cash earning for the family. As a matter of fact they primarily send their unmarried daughters and after that if there is no other alternative, send their wives also to work at the construction site.

In the Bhil society the unmarried girls are supposed as burden till they do not earn for their livelihood. If possible they arrange quickly for the marriage but due to shortage of money, many times they are unable to settle their daughters' marriage in time that is within 12 to 16 years of their age. So they always try to involve their daughters in some jobs to earn in cash and kind. They say that construction site is a very suitable place from where they can earn money easily. Moreover, they can get some extra benefits such as loan from their employers during their needs which is free from interest.

It is previously mentioned that at Udaipur there are married women come to work in construction site. It is probably due to the influence of city where the people have demand in all the aspects of materialistic life more in comparison to the village people so to meet their demands they have to earn more and more and in this way they even are somehow forced to send the married women also to earn cash. Moreover, in the city area they have the facilities of transport. These married women are never allowed to stay at the construction site during night and even till late hours. The husbands sometimes suspect and quarrel with them and dispute and murders related to the affairs at construction site are not so uncommon.

All those women studied belong to the families who are primarily the cultivators. It is mentioned earlier that in their field they are unable to produce sufficient crop. Most of them have dry, non-irrigated, less fertile land where they can cultivate only during rainy season. So they are forced to do other jobs to maintain their livelihood and construction work is preferred most by them. It gives them a regular income. The peak season for construction work—starts from November and lasts upto June (till the monsoon comes). During this period, it is easy for the contractors to accumulate labourers. During rainy season, all the cultivators families become busy to work in the field. So during the rainy season the labourers are not easily available for construction work but due to this the construction work does not suffer much as during rains construction work itself is also difficult. Due to shower the construction work also sometimes become impossible and it is forced to stop for sometimes.

Among 120 women 114 (95%) prefer to work in field. According to them in the field they can work freely and according to their capacity. There is no contractor, no mason, so supervisor to lead them throughout the day just like the bullock in the field. There is nobody to scold or to abuse them there. In the construction work, the employer, supervisor or his assistants never treat them as human being but always they are treated as machine. In the field a person can work with taking rests where in the construction site she has to work throughout the whole working hours. Generally these women labourers work as helpers to the mason. The masons do their work on contract basis but these women are engaged in daily wage basis. When a mason gets free from his work or completes his work or closes the day's work early, the women who works as helper with him is not freed, but immediately engaged by the supervisor to other works. She cannot avail the opportunity to take some rest during the remaining working hours. Inspite of having many disadvantages the women come to work as construction labourer when they have no work in the field. They prefer construction work than wood collection and selling, mud filling, etc. In all those jobs the earning is less than that in the construction work. Wood collection from jungle is a very laborious job. It is also informed by them that by this job they cannot earn sufficient. Sometimes they go to earn through the work of mud filling. But it is also not at all a profitable job. In this work a person has to fill mud in the vacant places in the hills from where the stone slabs are cut by the stone breakers. In mud filling work a person only can earn rupees four per day. For stone breaking and mud filling work there are contractors under whom the workers do the jobs of stone cutting and mud filling. Generally after the cultivating season the men folk go for stone breaking in the hills in groups. They call the village women to accompany as their helpers for mud filling purpose. Here actually the wage for mud filling is five rupees per day. But the men here work as mediator between the women and the contractor and they only pay rupees four per day to the women. In this way they (mediator) very commonly deprive the women of their actual wage. Sometimes they pay the money so late or even sometimes not pay a single coin. Moreover in that working site the men show very much conservativeness towards the women. The women cannot talk, laugh and discuss freely about their personal affairs. If any woman disobeys those men, it is immediately reported to her family members. The women said that they cannot even save a single coin from their own earnings for their personal use hiding from their family members as the whole village knows their wage.

Only except 6 (5%) women, all the women preferred cultivation. These 6 (5%) women preferred construction work to cultivation. They belong to the age group 16 to 25 and all are unmarried except one who is married. According to them construction work is the easiest way to earn a good amount.

Table 6 discusses the age group in which the women first started to come and join the construction work. Here in this table the women are divided into seven age group categories. It is observed from the table that maximum women started to come to work in the construction site in their age group 13-18 years. They are 46 (38.34%) in number. 33 (27.5%) women joined the work when they were below the age 13 years. 23 (19.17%) women joined the work when their age was between 19-23 years. With the increase of age the number is also decreased. There is no women found who joined after her 43 years of age. From the table it may be concluded that the women start to come to work in their very early age.

It is told by them that the contractors also prefer to recruit the young women as they are more efficient than the aged women. Even the children below 13 years are also recruited by the contractor as it is profitable for the contractor to recruit the children. The children are paid less but they do the same work as the aged persons do.

From Table 7 it is found that 77 (64.17%) women are attached first with the construction work with the person of same generation. 36 (30%) joined the work with the person of one generation above. Only 2 (1.66%) are found who joined first with their son or daughter, that is; the person one generation below and 5 (4.17%) of women attached themselves first at construction site alone.

Table 8 shows that at present also maximum number of women that is 81 (67.5%) come to work at the present site with the persons of the same generation. There are 27 (22.5%) women who come to work with the person of one generation above. 6 (5%) women are there who come to work with person of one generation below and also there are 6 (5%) women who come to work alone.

It is found from the Table 9 that largest number of women are attached first with the construction work through their consanguinal relatives. There are total 65 (54.17%) women who are brought by their consanguinal relatives for the first time. 37 (30.83%) women are there who are brought by some elderly person of the village or friends etc. 13 (10.83%) women are attached through their affinal kins.

Similarly from Table 10 of women coming with kins/or non kins at the present construction site, it is observed that maximum number that is, 58 (48.33%) of women come to work with their consanguinal kins. 39 (32.5%) of women come with their non-kins that is, either friend or village kins. 17 (14.17%) women are there who come with their affinal kins. Rest 6 (5%) women come to work alone at the construction site.

After discussing the Tables 4, 5(a), 5(b), 6, 7, 8, 9, 10, it can be said that in general the women first come to the construction site to work within 23 years of their age. They start to do construction work even before completion of their 12 years of age which is prohibited according to Labour Law. These women continue to work till their age of 53 years but maximum number of construction labourers belong to the age up to 33 years. Gradually it decreases. During this period women are with the maximum capability to do hardwork.

Maximum number of women come to work from the nuclear families and they are unmarried and majority of them are attached with the construction site for the first time with the person of their own generation.

The women workers who come alone to work at the construction sites, all come from the local villages which are very near to the construction site. It is found and also informed by them that women are not allowed to go alone to work at a construction site as migrant labourers. In all the cases the migrant labourers come to work with their husband, brother, sister, parents or elderly person of the village. It is found that in construction sites the women come in groups. The migrant labourers also come to work in a group leaded by an elderly male whose age is above 40. It is informed by them that the person must be an elderly influencial and important person in the village. In the Reliance Chemotex construction site the leader is found not to work, he only leads and activates the labourers whom he has brought to work. He gets his wage from the construction as a mate, not similar as the labourer.

At the Reliance Chemotex construction site 45 women labourers are interviewed. They are divided into six separate groups. The groups are of various sizes consisting of 4 to 20 persons. Some of the groups are under same contractor. The largest group is consisted of 20 persons coming from the villages named Rampur, Ratakhet and Dharicha. These villages are situated very close to one another. The women labourers from all these villages come to work with an influencial woman of village Ratakhet. They all work under the same contractor for several years. The influencial woman's name is Lali Bai. When there is any new work, the contractor sends his supervisor to village Ratakhet to meet with Lali Bai. He talks with her about the new work and offers her to join the work with her group. Then if she agrees, she talks with the women of her own village and of the neighbouring villages, who are willing to join the work, she also talks with their guardians and takes permission. After that she waits for the supervisor. The supervisor when comes, they finalise every thing such as wage, duration of work, transport, advance etc. and after that they join the work.

There is another group of women who come to work from a village which is very close to the construction site. They also come with a woman. The third group of women come in a large group of both the sexes under an old influencial man from the village Bilak. One of the supervisors under the contractor went to their village. There he met with the Panch Patel and with his help he was able to collect the group. Under the headship of an old man the group came and joined the construction work. There is a woman, who comes from another village named Baran, belongs to the same group.

There is a small group consisting of both the sexes who have come from a village named Kankroli. There are seven persons in total among them where there are two women. These women have come with their husbands. They are migrant labourers and among them only one woman is studied. (Another woman left the construction site earlier as she became ill).

Similarly another woman studied from a group of ten women. They are led by a man who is regarded as their mate. They have come through one supervisor from a village of Dungarpur district.

Lastly another woman is studied who have come as migrant labourer with her husband from a village in Mavli Tehsil of Udaipur district.

The rest 5 women studied at other construction sites at Udaipur, come from the neighbouring villages sometimes in group or sometimes alone to work. But they have definitely formed groups with the other labourers at the site.

70 women are studied at the Zawar Mines. 42 among them work at the K.K. construction site, 27 work at the Chowdhury construction site, one at the Mukherjee construction site. The groups are formed mainly according to the village from where they come to work, or rooms or blocks in which they are allotted their temporary shelter by the employer.

In case of K.K. construction site the women workers have taken their shelter in the newly built quarters. But they have not given permission to use any latrine of the newly built quarters. They have to go for in the nearby jungle for this purpose. The contractor usually allots three to four room for all those groups. Sometimes women change their own rooms with one another mutually. It is done as per their convenience and after getting the permission from the contractor. Generally the women prefer to stay with their friends or with the kins, or with the persons who come from the same village. These rooms are not so large where four persons can be accommodated. It is seen that in such a room atleast seven women are accommodated. So for staying they do not get sufficient space. The kitchen of those flats are too small where also atleast two to four persons are accommodated. So the women stay there very uncomfortably. There are 32 women migrant labourers of six groups stay in those newly built quarters.

The first group is consisted of seven women. Among them five come from the same village named Dhankabara; (Among them there are three sisters). The rest two women have come from two separate villages named Parsad and Leboda who have come with their other village persons and began to stay with the women of Dhankabara village in the same room and became so friendly with them.

The second group is consisted of sex women. They stay in the same room. Among them there are two sisters, two women from the same village and one woman with her niece.

There are four women who are accommodated in the kitchen where there is a woman with her niece and her two friends. They all are from the same village named Dhankabara.

There are three women from Bilak village got shelter in a room which is very close to the room of the men of the same village.

From Dhankabara village, another six women come who got their shelter in the same room. Among them also there are two sisters, aunt, niece and two other friends.

The sixth group of four women come from the village Baran who are accommodated in a separate small room.

The other two migrant women stay with their husbands in separate rooms.

The local labourers come from the neighbouring village such as Padla, Relan, Chanabda. They all have formed a large group after coming at the construction site.

At the Chowdhury construction site there are only eight migrant women labourers. They are accommodated in three huts (*jhupri*). One of these is alloted for a mother and her daughter. The second is for an elderly woman with three other women of the same village. The third room is allotted for one couple and the wife's sister.

Only one woman is studied at the Mukherjee construction site. The woman comes from the Dhankabara village.

Generally according to rule one woman should do her jobs for eight hours everyday. In case of work for excess time, the woman will get the benefit of doing overtime job.

The working hours at the Reliance Chemotex construction site are from 8.30 a.m. to 5 p.m. with a lunch break for half an hour (from 1.30 p.m. to 2 p.m.). But it is found that in practice all the women reach the site before 8 a.m. and are asked by the supervisor to start the work within 8 a.m.

It is informed by the women construction workers that the contractor made an agreement with them where he asks them to join or start the work within 8 a.m., half an hour earlier than the exact working hours with a promise, that they will be given extra time for half an hour during lunch hour that is lunch hour will start from 1 p.m. and which will be continued up to 2 p.m. But in practice the women never get this priviledge. During the field investigation it is observed that the women are allowed to take their lunch not before 1.30 p.m. but they are told it is as 1 p.m.

The contractor confessed that he does not tell the exact time for his own interest. It is true that the women are asked to start their work at about 8 a.m. but they cannot actually start work with in 8 a.m., and at the beginning they work very slowly. They cannot pick up the speed before 9 a.m. So to make up the loss of time or loss of progress he always tries to utilise them for more time.

The women workers at the Reliance Construction site prefer to get one hour lunch break as they have to do various types of works to do. During lunch break they take their food, clean utensils, go to the latrine, take some rest and chat among themselves.

In the Reliance Chemotex construction site the women are never released before 6 p.m. So they have to work at construction site for minimum nine and half a hour (approximately) daily. But it is not told to the women. These women cannot see the watch or time so they have to depend on the supervisor who never tells the exact time. In the construction site the mason do their job on contract basis so their work depends on the measurement instead of time. To increase the measurement of work done, that is, to earn more money they do not tell the correct time to their labourers. These women even sometimes knowing the exact time from others, cannot oppose so strongly as they are the casual labourers, who are appointed on oral agreement, can be terminated by the contractor at any moment. They only can appeal to or request the contractor to stop the work for the day, sometimes even they grumble but can never oppose strongly on this oppression.

There is no rest day or holiday except only on Holi, Diwali, Id, Independance day. But in all these holidays they do not get any wage. According to the Labour law six days in a week should be the working days and the seventh day should be the rest day but without pay. But in practice these women have to work throughout the week and do not get any rest day. They also do not like to get any rest day as rest day or holiday means they will not get the wage. So there is no rest day observed at the construction site.

In case of other construction sites at Udaipur it is also observed that the work starts from 8 a.m. and continues at least upto 5.30 p.m.

In Zawar Mines all the women have to be present within 8 a.m. and the working hours in Zawar Mines construction site is from 8 a.m. to 4 p.m., (though the actual working hour is from 8.30 a.m. to 5 p.m. with an interval of half an hour from 12 noon to 12.30 p.m.), without the lunch break from 12 noon to 12.30 p.m. But nobody is infact released before 6 p.m. They say that they never can reach their home before 7 p.m.

The women who come to work from the local villages of Zawar Mines, prefer to reach to their huts before the dusk as the road is non-mettalled and they have to go through the jungle crossing the hills. So the women made agreement with the contractor to start work before half an hour and to be released an hour earlier every day. The women also sacrificed the lunch break for half an hour with the demand that they should be released one hour earlier that is they will work from 8 a.m. to 4 p.m. Their demand is accepted by the contractor, but at the time of work he never follows the agreement which is made with those women and the women labourers informed that by this agreement the contractor himself is benefited. They say that instead of early start and sacrifice of lunch hour they cannot stop the day's work before 5.30 to 6 p.m. These women who come from the local villages have to cover atleast 10 kms. to reach their villages and they have to go through the jungle and crossing the hills. It is difficult for a person to go through those places when it becomes dark. But it does not mean anything to the contractors and generally they cannot stop the work earlier as per the agreement.

In construction work, there are masons who all are men. The women mainly work as the *jogandars* (helpers) of them. These women are locally called as *coolie*. They do the unskilled work. In the construction site along with them there are men also work as labourer.

These women labourers, locally known as *coolie* or *jogandar* do various types of works. They primarily assist the masons by supplying the concrete mixture. They carry those filling in a bowl known as *tagari* on their head. They assist the masons to erect a wall or to plaster a wall not only by supplying the concrete mixture but also by supplying the bricks, assist them holding the measuring implements at the time of measurement, by erecting temporary platform or ladder of bamboo and wood, which is locally known as *bhanra* on which the mason and labourer stand at the time of work at height. They water the newly constructed walls, wash the utensils and implements used during the time of work.

These women labourers beyond these works also do the work of *reti chhankna* (extraction of sand from stones, etc.). Many times they carry the big stone slabs from one place to another. They sweep or clean the floor. These women carry all the rubbish from a place where work of digging is done and throw it to some other place. Infact they perform all types of unskilled jobs in the construction site. Manytimes they do the job of preparation of concrete mixture locally which is known as masala. In fact it is the work of *belder* who are men. The wage of a *belder* is more than the wage of a woman labourer. Manytimes the women do the work of *belder* but not get any extra payment for that.

Men never like to do all the jobs which are done by the women labourers. They always try to work as *belder*. They think to work under a mason and to carry concrete mixture on head and to supply it to the mason is supposed very much derogatory type of job and holds less prestige. They do not want the mason to dominate on them and as a result often quarrels arise between the two. The masons also like or prefer to work with a woman helper instead of a man as they say the women are obedient and sincere in their work. They co-operate with the mason in each and every step of work. The women labourers rarely answer back and keep quite even at the extreme point of their tolerance. They are totally ignorant of labour law so that they get no benefit mentioned by the labour act. Due to their ignorance they always feel insecured and have a feeling that at any moment they may loose the job.

The *belders* prepare the concrete mixture, heavy stone slabs are carried by them from one place to another. The *belders* are treated as semi-skilled worker and the wage for them is seven rupees per day.

It is observed that at the Reliance construction site the drinking water is supplied to all the workers by a man who belong to the Brahman caste. The contractor engaged him for this work as the Brahmans hold the topmost position in Hindu caste hierarchy. In the construction site there are people from various castes and communities do the job. No body has objection to drink water from the hands of a Brahman. Due to this reason the contractor selected the person for that work. But at the Zawar Mines, drinking water for the unskilled labourers is carried by two women labourers belong to the Bhil community. Here all the unskilled labourers and some of the skilled labourers are from the same community. So they have no objection to drink water from them. The upper caste workers take water from a separate pot which is filled and carried by a Rajput worker. Here at the Zawar Mines there is no worker belong to the Brahman caste group.

According to the Labour Law children below 13 years of age should not do or be appointed at the construction site but inspite of having such a rule, specially in case of Reliance Chemotex construction site, there are several children do the work of unskilled labourer. They have to perform job equally with the women labourers of above 13 years of age. But they are paid much less. The children who work as labourers get only 80% of the actual wage of the unskilled labourers.

The women labourers at the small construction site do not get rupees five per day. Their usual rate they get rupees four per day with two cups of tea which costs fifty paise only. But at the time of payment it is written that they are paid rupees five per day and they have to give their thumb impression on the paper that they are paid rupees five per day. These women in most of the cases do not know the actual wage for their job. Sometimes they know that they are cheated by the contractors even then they accept it as they have no other alternative. They are illiterate, ignorant unorganized and even helpless and the employer takes this opportunity and as a result these women are exploited by the contractors in the form of underpayment.

On the other hand at the Reliance Chemotex construction site it is observed that most of the labourers get rupees five per day with the facility of free transport. The women who come to work from the nearby villages (which are within 1 km.) they only get rupees four per day. The contractors defend the discrimination by saying that all the women cannot do same work a day with same efficiency. The most efficient group is paid rupees five daily with transport facility. There are other two groups who are brought, from other tehsils and districts, by the contractor's own transport at the beginning of the construction work. They are regarded here as the migrant labourers. They have established temporarily their huts within 2 kms. from the construction site. They are paid five rupees per day.

In the Reliance Chemotex construction site the largest group among the labourers gets special preference and also priviledge as they are the oldest and most efficient group of women working under the same contractor. These women never go far to work as migrant labourer. They everyday come to work in the morning and after finishing the day's work, they go back to their village. It is atleast 7 kms. away from the village. It takes half an hour to fourty five minutes to reach the village by bus or truck. These women do not like to spend their earning on their travelling. So they made agreement for free transport. The contractor agreed to arrange for their transport and he arranged a transport to bring them everyday within 8 a.m.

At the Zawar Mines the wages are rupees five daily for adult labourers and rupees four for the children. The contractor here in this construction site cannot pay them less wage because there is a strong labour Union which is only membered by the labourers of mines but as the construction work is under the Mines authority who gave the contracts to the contractors, it may also help the construction labourers if they make some complaints against the contractor.

The women labourers generally are paid on monthly basis. At the small construction sites the informants told that they get payment on weekly or fortnightly. In case of the monthly payment it is never done before the seventh day of the month. In case of the Zawar Mines construction site monday is officially declared as holiday. But on the Monday if there is work, the contractor pays the days wage after finishing the day's work. He does not keep the record of Monday's work in the daily register. He keeps a separate register to keep the expenditure for the Monday's work.

The women labourers get an opportunity to take advance from the contractor in their need. The contractor has faith on them. They know the tribal labourers, specially the women never cheat. It is told that all the agreements and contracts are made verbally even they take loan without interest by verbal agreement. At the construction site when a woman comes to work with her friends she can spend her majority of time with those. She can spend the whole day joyfully with them. She does not feel so tired even after doing hardwork. They prefer to come to the construction site with their friends. Among their consanguinal Kin, they prefer to come with their sisters. At the Zawar Mines it is noticed that the young unmarried sisters work together till their marriage. Generally the eldest sister takes responsibilities to look after all the younger sisters at the construction site. After her marriage her place is taken by the sister next to her. When a woman comes with her parents or elder brothers or with mother-in-law, she has to work under the strict eyes of her guardians. She can not laugh and mix up with everybody at the site. Her movement, behaviour and relationship are restricted at the working site. She has to keep herself reserve and conservative. In such cases the parents always try to allot their working place very close to them by which they can keep their vigil on their sisters, daughter-in-laws, and daughters. In the Reliance Chemotex construction site there is a woman who comes to work with her mother-in-law. It is noticed that the mother-in-law always tries to work in a position very close to her. But as per the necessity of work, sometimes the contractor shifts them in other positions at a distance from one another. At that time the mother-in-law becomes very worried. She on such occasions requests the other women to safe guard her daughter-in-law. The daughter-in-law also knows this fact. So she never talks with men. She only does the work as directed by the employer.

When two sisters come to work, the elder one bosses the younger. She keeps all the responsibilities. She guides her younger sister how to behave with the people, what to do, how to protect herself from the happenings which their society does not tolerate. But sometimes in such a case the younger sister complains that the elder sister restricts her to enjoy freedom but she herself enjoys much freedom than the younger one.

They have informed that they do not like to work along with their relatives of their husband's side including their sister-in-laws (husband's sister and husband's brother's wife). The relationship between the two sister-in-laws in very rare cases is cordial and friendly. In such cases they help each other and discuss various types of problems faced by them in their families and also at the construction sites. But in general the sister-in-laws have feelings of rivalry, jealousy. Quarrels are very commonly occurred with each other.

At the Reliance Chemotex construction site there is a woman labourer named-Narayani Bai (30 years approx.) always tried to avoid her elder sister-in-law Bhamri Bai who is also found to work in the same site. It is told by Narayani that Bhamri is very quarrelsome and has a habit to complain against the village women including Narayani who come to work together at the construction site, to the villagers. There are several such instances which ultimately created problems for Narayani in her family. As for example, one day Narayani along with two other village girls was taking tobacco from a Sunni Muslim mason. Incidentally Bhamri reached there. They at that moment tried to hide tobacco inside their pockets. But she noticed all those and after returning village she went to complain against them. Narayani also could not escape from it and as a result she was brutally slapped by her husband infront of that woman. It is true that in the construction site offering of tobacco signifies the approach to have some illegal relationship. But side by side it is also true that the mason had no such intention. Another reason for objection is the man belongs to the Muslim community. Acceptance of food and drink and even tobacco from the hand of a Muslim is not permitted to them. According to Bhamri Bai, (45) (Narayani's elder sister-in-law) these women are young and do not know what should be done and what should not be. They very quickly get attracted to the masons and other skilled workers. These workers attract these women by offering tea or by visiting film or circus with them or to giving them presentations in cash or kind. In this way they attract these women and after that those women are in most of the cases exploited by those men. Being an elderly woman she thinks even inspite of having the mate, it is also her responsibility to keep those women under control to save them from those men.

The mate who brings the women to the construction site keeps overall supervision on the women. After the day's work he or she calls all the women and after collecting all the women they start for their village together. If anybody shows some irregular and indiscipline behaviour, at first the mate himself or herself warns the woman. The woman is given three to four chances to rectify herself even then if she does the same thing, then the mate informs it to her family.

When Kins come to work at the same construction site, they always have a feeling of mutual help and co-operation with each other. In all the cases the senior most Kin holds the responsibilities of all the Kins junior to him or her.

Even when the women come to work with their friends and other villagers, they also help each other.

In case of pregnancy, a woman labourer hides it from the contractor till she can. They have informed that the contractors do not like to engage a pregnant woman in the work to avoid hazards as it is risky for a pregnant woman to do such labourious job. Even then if any woman works, she is not given any priviledge for her such condition and she always told that the contractor will not be responsible if she gets troubles even during her work at the construction site. She is doing the work as per her wishes, therefore, all the responsibilities will go to the woman. But always the contractors avoid to engage such women.

These women do not get any facility of maternity leave if they continuously do the work even during the eighth month of the pregnancy. They are always the daily wage lobourers, do the work on no work no pay basis in the construction site.

In the construction site the women labourers are not given any facility or priviledges.

There is no separate resting place for them. They do not get any toilet and bathroom facility, even the women who bring their small breast feeding children get no separate place to keep their small children. Generally such a woman brings her baby wrapping by a cloth, then she keeps the child in a *tokri* (basket) generally at a corner near to her working place. Lactating women get a very little time after long intervals to feed the children. But the contractors do not like to give them much time. So most of the times the women cannot feed the children as much as they want. Sometimes they feed such children hiding from the contractors and the supervisors.

In the construction site there are several groups of women who come to work from the different places. It is found that rivalry, jealousy, competition and even friendship is found among the groups. Rivalry and jealousy comes between two groups when a group of women are seen to get priviledges in wage, preference in work, etc. from the contractors, masons and supervisors. These women also feel curiosity to know about the women of other groups.

In the Reliance Chemotex construction site among all the groups the largest group known as Lali's group get more priviledges than the other groups. It is the oldest group to the contractor who are attached with the contractor from several years. They always try to get maximum benefit, importance from the contractor. They get more wage, transport facilities and even the advance money (whenever they ask for it to the contractor). They have a tendency to dominate over all other groups of women. In that construction site the supervisor brought another group of young women who belong to the age group between 16 years to 25 years. They are unmarried young and also attractive. So many times the contractors, supervisors and the masons show interest on those women and as a result give some priviledges to them. This not liked by the Lali's group. They always try to show negligence to those women. On the other hand those women try to make friendship with Lali's group but Lali and other women of her group do not entertain those women. They always try to show that these women are not so efficient like them. Those young women wear *Kabja* (blouse with short length which only covers the upper half portion of the breast). The women of Lali's group wear *polka* (the blouse with long length, which is long upto the waist of the women). One day one woman of Lali's group told that she feels shy as these women show half of their breasts. This is a shame for the women which attracts the men working in the site. Generally the Bhils women wear either *Kabja* or *polka*. In general they have no such feeling of shame for keeping the half portion of the breast open when they wear *Kabja*. It is probably the influence of urban life which makes the girl to feel shame.

The third group of women come from the village named Kanpur are not such hard working and efficient like Lali's group. They are paid four rupees per day per head as their wage less than the wage paid to Lali and her group. It is observed that the women of this group always try to keep good relationship with women of Lali's group. Lali's group of women are also helpful to them.

When a woman worker gets her month menstrual cycle, she informs it to the group leader to arrange some easy work for her as *reti chhankna* (separating sand from stones, etc.), work of *pani pilana* (watering of newly built structure). They try to avoid heavy work as carrying of heavy load upon head, lifting it, or work at the upstairs.

These women help each other in their need. Even they also take loan from each other.

In the Reliance Chemotex site the migrant labourers who come to work in a group are generally accommodated in the nearby villages. They buy *ata* (wheat) from the shop in the village, prepare their *roti* (hand made bread) separately. When a woman comes with any of her Kins, they prepare their *roti* separately, but the *sabjji* is cooked jointly with others.

At the Zawar Mines the men are accommodated separately from the women but they are permitted to take food with any group of women according to their convenience. They may be of the same group from the same village or they have got a very friendly relationship with each other after coming to the work at the construction site. The women of a group cook rotationally, bring water, wash utensils. The men of the group do not help in those work. They only help in shopping, and to bring fuel from jungle. These women, at the time of coming to work at the construction site bring their own *ata* (wheat) from their own village. They prepare their own *roti* (hand made bread) separately and the *sabjji* is prepared collectively. Those women informed that the men who eat with them supply their *ata* (wheat) to any of the women who prepares *roti* (hand made bread) for them.

These women construction labourers take food twice a day, once during the lunch time at the working site and the other during night after returning home from the construction site. Sometimes they take their breakfast with tea and *roti* before coming to the construction site. Those who take *roti* in the morning do not take any lunch.

The local labourers at the Reliance Chemotex construction site who come to work everyday early in the morning take tea in the morning and carry lunch box with them and swallow lunch during daytime and at night take dinner after returning home.

During lunch hours women workers get a few minutes rest. At first they wash their hands and collect their tiffin carrier boxes which they usually hang on the branches of a big tree or keeps at a corner of the working site. Some of them bring the lunch by wrapping with a dirty torn cloth. They sit in groups at their own selected places, some of them sit inside a room, some in front of the building under the shadow of the tree. Those who do not bring tiffin also sit with other women at that place, gossip and take some rest. Those who bring the food, open their tiffin carrier so hurriedly and take food without missing even a second. Generally they bring two to three thick chapati/roti of jawar or maize which are taken sometimes with sabjji, sometimes with pickles or sometimes even with some salt, onion and chhili powder. They cannot afford for sabjji everyday. They remain so hungry and just swallow their food. A mother even never waits for her daughters and it is same for the daughter. Those who come from the same family, the two bring the food together in the same tiffin carrier. Each of them takes her share from the tiffin carrier. If her hunger remains, then also, she never takes from the other's share. But if two, who share from the same tiffin carrier, eat together, then if one of them notices that the other is remain hungry then she offers some from her own share. The women of the same group offer vegetables to each other. After taking the food they drink water, then they wash their utensils and after that come to the place, begin to gossip generally lying down or sitting on the floor spreading the torn cloth which they keep on head as a buffer on which they keep the heavy *tagari* (the big convex bowl on which a woman labourer keeps the cement mixture and carry those). Generally the older persons go to sleep. The younger ones play, go to the toilet, gossip at the tea shop close to the construction site. This is the time specially to go to the latrine. During working hours generally the supervisor does not want to give them time to go to the toilet. So they try to get fresh during this time. The younger ones play, joke with each other, lough and enjoy some freedom during this time. The parturient mothers go to sleep, those who come to work with babies, nurse their babies, keeping on lap. This is the time for taking food, for taking rest, to get themselves fresh. They comb their hair, put *bindi* on forehead, and *Kajal* to eyes. One of the important tasks during lunch hour is to detect lice from each other's head. When they go to the toilet they use their tiffin carriers to carry water for defication. They urinate in the construction site but in case of the Zawar Mines they cannot urinate in the construction site. For that they have to go outside.

The migrant women at the K.K. construction site at Zawar Mines during lunch hour come to their room, gather together and take their own food. When a wife comes to work with her husband, it is observed that they do not like to waste their time by gossiping with others. They do their own works such as cleaning, washing and take some rest. Those who come as local labourers, generally do not bring food. Those who bring food, eat separately sitting at a corner of the construction site.

The women there also spend the lunch hour after taking the meal, by taking some rest, talking and discussing their problems, and by cleaning and washing. The group of women who do not want to take the priviledges of lunch hour, remain busy with their works during the lunch hour. They are asked to do *reti chhankna*, to water the newly constructed walls, etc.

In all the construction sites they mainly talk about the hard work which they have to do, about the attitude of the contractors, supervisors towards them and how the contractors and the supervisors behave with them. It is a very common phenomena that they make complains, against the supervisor, the contractor, and sometimes even against the masons for their illtreatment towards them. They complain to their team leader, who is commonly known as mate. The mate through proper channel asks for justice. They like to talk about their personal life, their families. They also like to talk about their village, village elders, about their works for the development of their village. They talk on adultery, pre and post marital sex relationship of the women of the village. A woman discusses her personal life and problems at home or in the working site. They are very much fond of discussing about the women of the other groups and their relationship with the supervisors, contractors, masons and all the males attached with the construction site. They talk about their food, economic conditions, about the market, cost of things, about their saris, jewellary, cinemas and circus. They often go to visit cinema.

The non-tribal labourers specially the women never exchange their food with these tribal women labourers even in case of deep friendship with them. They take their food separately sitting at a distance from the tribal women.

Quarrel between the women labourers is not uncommon but they solve it easily. The issues of the quarrels are their own personal affairs, about the load of work, the preference given to any of the women by the contractor or supervisor. In case of adultery, pre or post marital relationship with the persons attached with the construction work, the other women take it as an offence to their own society and take it very seriously. They discuss the matter among themselves and complains to their guardians. Centering such type of issues quarrels are very common.

It is also marked that the women labourers who come from distant places as the migrant labourers do not behave so freely with the men of other groups. They are not allowed to make intimate relationship with the persons of other groups. Inspite of having such restrictions there are cases where a woman is found to have a pre marital or extra marital illegal sex relationship for which these women are even beaten brutally. The women who come from the local villages enjoy freedom in comparison with the migrant women labourers to make friendship with the men in the construction site.

The women workers above the age of 40 years do not usually talk with men. They even do not like the freedom enjoyed by the younger women at the construction site. Often they scold, make complains against those women. On the other hand the men attached with the same work do not get much interest to talk with those aged women. They always want or prefer to make friendship with the younger women. The young women generally like to talk, gossip, lough, play and make friendship which sometimes grow in very intimate relationship. There are several such cases for which they face problems in their society. Even then these women cannot restrict themselves from the attraction of the men working in the same construction site. Sometimes it ends in life partnership also. There are several such cases. When the boy and the girl belong to the same community, that is, Bhil, then generally no objection is raised by any of the party sometimes even the parents and relatives arrange to settle their marriage but when the boy and the girl feel that there may be objection raised on their marriage, then the couple runs away from the site and begins to live as husband and wife. In such a case, the girl's party goes in search of their own daughter to the boy's village where they meet with the boy's party. They generally go with an attitude to bring back their own daughter. If the boy's party accepts the girl as the boy's wife, and refuses them to give their girl back, then they have to pay an amount as *jhagda*. Among the Bhils there is a system of paying bride price at the time of marrige. If anybody elopes with a woman, he has to pay *jhagda* (compensation) to the girl's family. The amount is settled at the presence of village elders. Customarily the girl is not allowed to visit her parental village till her husband pays the whole amount. Marriage by elopement is known as *urake le aya or uthake.*

There are seven such cases at the studied construction sites. In all the cases the girls and the boys belong to the same community. But if the man belongs to other community, then the case is different. The Bhils do not perfer to marry outside their own community. In case of marriage outside the community which is customarily forbidden, the girl's family is outcasted. A heavy punishment is imposed on them by the society.

Women sometimes get sexually involved with the men at the construction site just to earn some extra money and even only for some enjoyment. They make friendship, intimacy and even illegal sex relationship with those men. Those are not entertained by their society. The women in maximum cases make such type of relationship just to earn some extra money or to get some presentations and to visit the cinema, circus and to eat some delicious food, tea and for some enjoyment. In their society the unmarried women are free even to keep pre marital sex relationship with the persons even outside their own community until and unless they get pregnant. Though it is not illegal yet it is not liked or encouraged in the Bhil society.

When a woman comes to work with her any family members and specially with the husband, the husband prefers to work along with his wife or at a close distance with her. It sometimes creats problem in the construction site. The husband always tries to help his wife sometimes even neglecting their own work. In such cases the supervisor, the contractor get irritated with them and change their position of work.

In each and every construction site the women labourers are always noticed afraid of the contractor. They feel shy and hesitant to talk with him. But it is very interesting to note that the contractors in most of the cases have least interaction with the women labourers. If they feel to say something to the women labourers, say it through some of the assistants. In rare cases if a contractor tells something to any of the women labourers he generally addresses them as *mataji*, *bahinji*, or *baiji*. The young women are addressed as *chhori* which is a very common term for those women.

The supervisors and the petty contractors have direct dealings with the workers. They are the representatives of the contractors. It is not possible for a contractor to look after all the works throughout the day. The contractors keep several assistants such as petty contractor, supervisor, mate, etc. to maintain the work. The contractor himself is the overall incharge in a construction site under whom these supervisors, petty contractors work. In such a situation the women can directly interact with those person instead of the contractor. These supervisors or petty contractors also know each and every worker by name who work under him which is not at all possible for a contractor. The women workers are seen to talk freely with them. The women sometimes tell them all about their difficulties and problems they faced during the work generally through their leader and request to give some facilities in work. In their need these women labourers take loan from the construction site through these supervisors, petty contractors and mates. During the field investigation it is noticed that once to make the women happy, one of the supervisors gave half day leave (without cutting the wage) to his group of labourers. They appealed for it to go to visit cinema or circus and the supervisor agreed. Though it is very rare yet sometimes these women are given such type of incentives to break the monotony of work. The supervisor told that he will meet up his loss for that half day by getting more works from the women in some other days.

The women labourers argued that these supervisors and the petty contractors are very intelligent. They know how to exploit these women or how to get more and more work from these women. All the times they drive the workers for quick work. They treat these women as mechine. The women told that some of the contractors, supervisors, etc. are with very bad temperament. It is very difficult for them to work with such types of employers.

Generally nobody likes to work on the overtime basis. They always try to avoid to do overtime job. But sometimes they have to do work as they are forced by the supervisor or the petty contractors. In case of the men when they are asked to do the overtime job, they never work sincerely. Within half an hour they begin to cry to stop the work. But the women labourers cannot force the contractor as the men do to stop the work. They feel hesitant to talk those persons. They are very much scared of them. They always feel hesitant to ask for some favour for them. They feel always scared that they may be terminated anytime at any moment. The supervisor and the petty contractors also know this fact and take this opportunity to force the women to do overtime jobs. The male labourers specially the non-tribals sometimes try to oppose. Once during the field investigation at the Reliance Chemotex construction site it is observed that the contractor asked the labourers to work on overtime. They asked both tribal and non-tribal labourers to do the job. But the non-tribal labourers formed a small group to oppose against the overtime job. The supervisor even the contractor requested them for several times but they ignored, atlast they agreed to work when the contractor promised them to pay extra for a film.

Similarly, once at the Zawar Mines, while the labourers after finishing the day's work were washing their implements, the contractor ordered them to work on overtime basis on that day for there was an urgent meeting to be held on the next day by the Mines authority who would come to see the progress of work. Excepting an old labourer all the men left the place ignoring the contractor. But the women could not escape. They appealed that their family members shall scold them if they return so late but the contractor ignored it and forced them to do the work.

There is another case observed during the field investigation. The contractor once asked all the women labourers both tribal and non-tribal to work on overtime basis. The women were unhappy with that order. It was already late to return to their village. But nobody could argue with the contractor. The work started at about 6 p.m. The tribal women started to work fast but the non-tribal women grumbled among themselves ignoring the contractor. They worked very slowly and less job is done by themselves. After an hour one of the non-tribal aged women told that they were so tired, could not work more. The supervisor and the contractor requested them to work and told them that he would offer tea to them if they could finish the whole work. Then those women were happy. Again after few minutes these non-tribal women asked for water. The Brahman carried water. Firstly the non-tribal women drank. Then the tribal women got the opportunity to quench their thirst. When the non-tribals were drinking water, a young tribal girl of 10/11 years of age, attached with the work asked for water. The contractor scold her and asked her to wait till the non-tribals women drink water. The work continued till 8.30 p.m. Then the non-tribals were offered tea. The tribals were not even asked. The groups of tribal women were in hurry to reach home. They even did not wait for the payment of overtime wage.

Following day when the tribal women came to work, they requested their group leader to tell the supervisor not to ask them to work after their day's work. They were very much displeased with the supervisor, contractor and also with the petty contractor for the difference of attitude and behaviour with the non-tribal women. But they are not so strong to oppose against it.

The tribal women labourers told that if they reach late, they have to face several questions from the family members and even from the villagers. The villagers never believe that these women speak the truth; the family members also suspect and scold and even sometimes beat them. It is also told by them that after finishing the day's work they feel so tired, they sometimes even do not feel to cook food. So they do not like to do overtime job, which seems beyond their limit. Their health do not permit to do the overtime job. They get headache, they suffer from body pain. After doing overtime job they do not feel to come to work on the following morning, but even then they have to come and join the work. They told that they are serving the same contractor for seven/eight years. They get preference than the other tribal women labourers but the non-tribal women get facilities and preference even they do less work.

When the work at a construction site is finished, the women sometimes get work under the same contractor in some other area or under different contractor in different construction site. Till they get the job or in between these two works the women take rest, go to their villages (in case of the migrant labourers), visit relatives in the neighbouring villages and keep contact with their leader to get engaged in some other construction site. Till they get any employment at other construction site, they do certain other job to earn the livelihood.

Discussion

The chapter women at work mainly discusses how, why, when and with whom the Bhil women come to work in the construction site. The author tried to draw a brief sketch of their daily life in the construction site, their relationship with others, their wage, payment facilities and priviledges they are given etc.

It is observed that all of these women construction workers belong to the cultivating families who also prefer to do the works associated with cultivation. But they have not enough land to produce sufficient crop to maintain the livelihood throughout the year. Moreover their lands are non-irrigated and less fertile. They only can produce crop during the rainy season. Rest of the part of the year they hardly can produce crop and even it is difficult to get any work associated with cultivation in other's land. In this situation necessity forces them to get attached with construction work and only except rainy season they do various types of jobs such as wood cutting, mud filling, construction work etc., of which construction work is preferred most among those.

In general women come to be attached with construction work at their very early age. They even start the work before completion of their 12 years of age which is prohibited in the labour law. The women even continues to work till their age around 50 years but it depends on their health condition. The contractors and the supervisors, etc. do not want to appoint the women above 40 years (approximately). They prefer to engage young and healthy women in such a manual labour. It is found that maximum number of women belong to the age up to 35 years.

Economic condition forces the women construction labourers come to get attached with the construction site at their very early ages. They are generally brought by persons of one generation above or come along with the elderly members of same generation, sometimes with friends. They in general come to work with their friends and the persons of same generation under the guidance of a senior and influencial person who is regarded as their mate. These women labourers in maximum cases are observed that come from the nuclear families. In the present study the labourers belong to two categories that is, the local and the migrant labourers. Some of the labourers come everyday from their villages early in the morning and return everyday after completion of the day's work. They are called as local labourers. Other labourers who come from distant villages shift temporarily to the construction site from their own village and stay there till the work is completed. They are called as migrant labourers. In the construction sites at Udaipur the number of local labourers is more than the migrant labourers but in the Zawar Mines the migrant labourers are more than the local labourers. In both the cases among the women labourer unmarried girls are more in number. It is told by them that they do not like to send their women specially the married women to work in the construction site. But contradictions noticed in case of the local labourers at Udaipur. There the number of the married women workers is more than the unmarried women. They put their argument for this contradiction. But in short one can come to conclusion that it is probably due to the influence of urban life which made them less rigid in this matter in comparison to the construction workers at the Zawar Mines. These women at Udaipur only are permitted to work as local labourers not allowed to go and stay at the work site as the migrant labourers.

They argued that only due to economic constraints they are forced to come to work to the construction site. Otherwise they would not be allowed to come and join the construction work. Even when they are send, they are not send alone. They are always send in a group under the headship of some responsible person.

In the construction site those who work as migrant labourers, generally the authority arranges for their temporary settlement. The women labourers according to the rule have to work for eight hours daily with a lunch break for half an hour. Incidentally in no case it is strictly followed. In all the cases everyday they have to work more for which no excess money is paid to them. They are never told the correct time. They are rather exploited even for one to one and half an hour daily.

The main work or the women labourers is to assist the masons. Beside this other works are to water the newly built structure, mud felling, and the work of reti chhankna. Sometimes they also do the works of bleder for which they do not get any extra amount for that. Actually the Beleders get the wage of semi-skilled labourer and the wage is more.

In case of unskilled women construction labourers as per rule the wage is Rs. 5 per day. But in many cases they are not paid the actual amount. In many cases they are paid less. This is the another point of exploitation.

Their payment is made on weekly or fortnightly or on monthly basis. They work on no work no pay basis. They are not elligible to enjoy any leave or holiday with pay. They are not given any maternity leave or any leave on medical ground. In the construction site only facility is that they can take loan from the employer without interest.

A construction site becomes busy just after the sun rise. Gradually the workers accumulate to the site, they start the day's work. The women workers also accumulate at the work site. At first they keep their tiffin or lunch box at a safe place, then drink water and quickly prepare themselves ready for work. They keep their small piece of cloth on head making it in a round shape which work as buffer on which they put heavy *tagari* full with concrete mixture. They collect the concrete mixture and supply it to their respective masons. This is repeated till the lunch break. They are not allowed to waste a moment without doing the job. Even then the supervisor or petty contractor scold them to get more speed. They are driven by those persons throughout the work to do the job faster and faster. Lunch break is only the time when they can take some rest. They feel so hungry and so tired, feel the time for lunch break is too small. But manytimes they are ready to sacrifice this period also only with a hope that they can reach the village half and hour earlier. In this point also they are exploited. Knowingly or unknowingly they do not bother much for those exploitations. Sometimes they grumble but for a few moments. They know there is no gain to oppose the employer. They many loose the job. So it is better to request some favour from them instead of having quarrels. It is better to do the work peacefully as their families are in need of their earning.

It is very astonishing to see that after doing such arduous labour the young women remain so energetic. They continue to lough, play and sing throughout the day till the dusk, side by side performing such heavy works. What is the source of their energy? They take insufficient food. They can not get much time for rest then how they get such energy? The young women replied they also feel tired, they suffer from body pain but to forget all those they try to keep them enjoying. Otherwise they would not be able to do such arduous and monotonous job.

4

Women in the Home

A home is the pivot of the society and a woman is its centre. The home here signifies the family which is the basic unit of their society. It teaches a person from very early childhood how to adjust in the family and in broader spectrum in the society through the rules and regulations or norms and behaviour of the society. It helps a person to make a self image to have self identification. It is very important to study the role played by woman and her position in the family, beside studying their role and position at the construction site. Here it is discussed in the following lines through their following states of life (citing some cases).

(a) As a grown up unmarried daughter.

(b) As a wife.

(c) As a daughter-in-law.

(d) As a mother-in-law.

(e) As a widow.

(f) As a separated/divorced woman.

(a) As a Grown up Unmarried Daughter

The unmarried grown up women are supposed to be the major working hands for the family. The family is largely dependent on their earnings from the construction work and beside this their work is also needed in their families. In most of the cases the Bhil families are of nuclear type where the mother often gets busy with her child care specially with the nursing of the newly born baby. Sometimes they cannot work hard due to pregnancy or delivery. When a mother is in such a state of her life, then the unmarried grown up girl has to take the burden of the work load of the family. She is not excused for the heavy and tiring works she has to do in the construction site and has to perform a large portion of the household work before coming to the construction site. Right from the morning till night she has to do a lot of work without taking much rest. As an earning source she is not given any priviledge or preference to do less work, to take more food or to take more rest in comparison with others. On the contrary they have to work more and more for the family.

Tulsi Bai (15 years) come to work from the village with her aunt. She is an unmarried woman of marriageable age. She has three brothers and two sisters, the youngest one being just one month old. So her mother has to be engaged with the little child for most of the time. Moreover she can not work hard due to her weakness. So Tulsi has to do all her household works before coming to the construction site.

Early in the morning, before anyone else she leaves the bed, sweeps the floor, gets herself fresh. After that she fetches water from the village well and prepares sabjji and roti. Sometimes she prepares tea and offers to her parents. She herself takes tea on occasions if she gets any time to take tea. Then she takes her lunch packet with her and then leaves for the construction site.

While she is away to the construction site, her mother cleans the room, gives food to the family members. Uncleaned utensils are washed by her.

After day's work she hurriedly reaches home, cleans utensils if there is any left for her, fetches water and occasionally cooks food. She distributes food to everybody, and after taking food she cleans utensils and then finally goes to sleep.

They use firewood as their fuel. When the fuel is needed, Tulsi goes to jungle; collects and brings it. Generally once in fifteen days she goes to collect wood. On that day she does not go to work to the construction site.

Sometimes when she returns home late her mother cooks the food. Family members take food without waiting for Tulsi, for whom the mother keeps the Khana or food. When she reaches home all except her parents go asleep.

Her mother is physically weak so cannot work hard so she has to work in the home even when she is so tired. Inspite of having such health condition her mother tries to share her load of work as much as she can. Tulsi's father is a stone breaker and has to do the hard work, hence he does not like to help his wife and daughter in household work. After he takes his night's meal, he chats with the village persons of his age and takes some rest. Only he does the work of shopping to buy all the consumable articles like vegetables, cereals, oil, salt from Baniya in loan, if there is no money at hand, the shopping is sometimes done by Tulsi and her brother.

She gets only 7 to 8 hours for taking rest at night which seems not sufficient for her. Her body aches throughout the day. She feels so sleepy all the time.

She is never appreciated by her father. She thinks that he expects more and more money from her. But her mother understands her problems and tries to give her relief. Her mother is not able to perform heavy duties even then she tries to help her. But when there is some delicious food item the large portion of it is distributed to her father and younger siblings. Rest-portion of it is taken by her mother and herself.

She approximately earns rupees one hundred and fifty only per month. But she hardly can keep rupees five for her personal expenditure, which is not sufficient as hand expenses throughout the whole month.

Inspite of such sincerity and hard work, her parents on occasions suspect her on her character. They scold her. She bears it and when she fails to bear any more, she retaliates; and as a consequence she is beaten by her parents.

The cases of growing unmarried women are several and there are variations also. But it is found that in all the cases the family wants more and more from them. They are regarded as one of the main working and earning source of the family and in all the cases it is found that they are less permitted to spend their earnings as per their wishes.

(b) As a Working Wife

The married women who come to work are mainly from the nuclear families. It is observed that the husband do not prefer to send their wives to work in the construction site specially as local labourer. Generally the wives come to work as migrant labourer with their husbands, brothers, sons and daughters or some very close Kins. Here is no married woman who comes to work at the Zawar Mines from local village.

At Udaipur among 50 women, 21 married women come to work from the local villages. Previously it is mentioned it may be due to the effect of urbanization, the people in and around Udaipur changed their ideas to some extent and began to send their wives and daughter-in-laws to work at the construction site. When the married women are sent to work they are mainly sent for betterment of their family conditions through their earnings. Though they earn money for their families yet they do not get any extra priviledge or preference from the family side by getting some extra food, or by getting importance in maintaining the family budget. They are not permitted to keep the hand expense as per their wish. On the other hand in most of the cases it is found that their husbands get so suspicious of their wive's characters. Sometimes women do not get sufficient time to work in the household, their family members come dissatisfied with them due to this.

Bhamri Bai (28) a woman comes to work with the other elderly women of the same village. She is regarded as the main earning source in their family of three members; that is, she with her husband and only five months old son. Her husband is a sick person, he cannot work hard. Generally he works in their own field during the rainy season and as agricultural labourer in others' field. She has to do all the works at home—fetching water, cleaning utensils, washing clothes, cooking and with all these most of the works of child care. Her husband never helps her. Instead, by any chance if she cooks food which are not so tasty, then those are thrown away by her husband. If she tries to keep a little amount of money as her hand expenses, those are snatched by him. The man always suspects his wife in each and every aspect. He does not trust his wife. Bhamri has to bear all his ill treatments as she loves him and cannot think of living without him.

It is true that there are several cases where the married women are involved in some relations with men of other caste and communities which are socially not permitted or even tolerated. Due to this reason in the families of most of such married women have to face suspicion, quarrels, which results disturbances in the married life. There are cases where married women construction labourers were involved in love with men construction workers and ran away with such persons leaving the family, husband and even children. Due to such happenings do not like to send their wives to work in the construction site and even when they are sent due to economic need very often crisis in their marital life happens.

These women inspite of having their own earnings, hardly can save some from their earnings for their personal expenditure (that is to buy bangles, tobacoo etc.). Sometimes they are consulted by their husbands how to maintain the family budget but most of the time their husbands' opinion is final.

(c) As a Working Daughter-in-law

Generally a daughter-in-law has no separate identity in her in-laws house even when she is an earner. She is expected to be submissive and obedient. When she gets her wage, certainly she has to pay it to her husband or the father-in-law or the mother-in-law who maintains the family budget. She does not get priviledge to visit her parents whenever she wishes. She has to seek permission for that.

Narayani Bai's (32) mother-in-law works at a different construction site. She asked Narayani to join that construction site with her. Narayani does not want to work with her in the same construction site. She thinks minimum freedom she would not get in her working place if she works with her in the same construction site. She is attached with a construction site close to their village where the work of private building construction is going on. Due to this reason, her mother-in-law is not pleased with her. She always tries to instricate her son to suspect and scold his wife. Her husband is not so rude to her and most of the times tries to ignore such types of gossips. Even then sometimes he gets angry with her as a result they quarrel with each other.

Her mother-in-law generally does not work much when she is at home. Lion's share of the day's work is done by Narayani.

Narayani earns rupees one hundred and twenty only (approximately) per month. She has no right to keep some amount from her earning. Whenever she needs to buy a sari or blouse or ghaghra or bangles etc. she has to ask for it to her husband.

(d) As a Working Mother-in-law

Generally the position of the working mother-in-law is much better than the working daughter-in-law. The working mother-in-law is not suspected. She can keep an amount from her earning and after coming home she gets food ready for her. She has to work less in the house.

Etoyari Bai (45 years) and her daughter-in-law work at the same construction site. Etoyari generally does less work at home, gets a very prestigious position there. Her daughter-in-law cooks food and does most of the household work. Etoyari only assists her. In the family she is a proud woman, having money in hand. But she does not encourage the daughter-in-law to keep some money from her own earnings. Etoyari can visit her relatives whenever she wishes but her daughter-in-law cannot do so.

(e) As a Working Widow

The widows studied live separately either alone or with their children. Such a woman has nobody who can scold her, beat or behave so cruely with her. A widow spends her earnings as per the necessity. There are two widows studied who leave alone, informed that they are happy with their jobs and earnings. They always try to save some money from their earnings for the future. There is a widow lives with her two sons. In her case she cannot save a single amount for the future. Her earned amount is not sufficient to maintain the family and to repay the loan. She had taken loan from a Baniya at the time of her daughter's marriage (at that time she was not attached with the construction work).

These guardianless women on the other hand face several types of problems. They are sometimes cheated by the villagers and kinsmen, many times the young widow construction workers become the centre of gossips.

Dulki Bai (45 years) has two bighas of land where she grows *makki* (maize). She has no working hand to cultivate the land. She has to hire labourer whom she has to pay. For this purpose every year she spends a lot of money for cultivation during rainy season. There is no guarantee that the crop production will be profitable. She says that if she had a male working hand in the family then she would not hire labour and she would have been benefited. She is a working woman. So her villagers always try to get more profit from her. During working period in field, she has to stop coming to the construction site. Otherwise her hired hand cheats her. She has to supervise the work in her fields.

PHOTOGRAPH

2. Mate with her labourers

3. Chit-chat during recess

4. Group of Informants in the site

5. In lieu of bread to carry heavy concrete mixture

6. Joyful attitude and strenous work by tribal women labourer

7. In search of alternatives—The tribal women during their arduous labour

The another woman Lali Bai (38 years) has a daughter who is married to a stone breaker two years before. Lali is very much unhappy with her son-in-law. He never allows his wife to visit Lali because Lali is a construction worker. Instead he meets Lali and demands money for her. He often tells his wife against Lali that Lali is with a very bad character. When Lali arranged her marriage with the man that time also there was no objection for her job at construction site. He has no objection and often demands money from her which comes from construction site. He never asks her to stay with him or he does not want to stay with her or to look after her. She has no other alternative to earn her livelihood. She was forced to sell all her property after her husband's death. She had not go for remarriage. She brought up her only child and settled her life by arranging her marriage. All these are done by her earning from construction site. She is very much annoyed with the man for this. She agreed that she mixes with the men working in the same construction site, even she is very intimate with the mate but she has no illegal relation with any person working in the same construction site.

According to her it is so easy to tell many such type of gossips against a widow because a widow is a helpless person. In maximum cases those gossips are not true.

(f) As a Separated/Divorced Working Woman

Separated and divorced women among them are the most helpless women. In most of the cases they stay with their parents. They are sometimes treated as burden. So they come to work to earn their livelihood. They say when they stay with their parents, they get more comfort than to live with their brothers' families. A divorced woman is treated as an outsider. Nobody in the family asks for their advise how to run the family. Nobody likes them to stay for a long time with that family. As an unimportant person of the family they pass their days and always has a tendency to get some job to earn her livelihood till she remarries. So she gets easily attracted to the construction work labour or any other non-skilled sector. The villagers in general have a suspect on the construction workers. These women also cannot escape from it and they are suspected more as they are divorce or separated.

Therefore it is seen in the chapter that in all the cases the women construction labourers get no special preference as an earner. The family does not hesitate to take the earning from the construction site but always these women are suspected.

These women have to perform the household works at home. The burden is more on the unmarried and young married women.

These women are hardly asked for their decisions to run the family. Even they are asked, their decisions are mostly ignored.

Inspite of earning a lucrative amount these women hardly can keep a share from it for their personal uses. Their guardians do not like that. Whenever they need some money to buy something or to spend elsewhere, they have to ask for it to the guardian and he according to his convenience meets her demand.

5

Opinion Survey

Opinion regarding the women construction labourers is taken from the contractors, supervisors, masons, men labourers with whom the women have to work daily at the construction site. Along with their opinion, opinion from the villagers from which villages the women come, are also taken. Some of those are written below :—

(A) Contractors

Contractor 1. He[1] is very much ignorant of the women labourers working under him. He even cannot tell their names except the important ones like Lali. He told that due to shortage of time, he appointed supervisors and petty contractors who may give some information on the women.

1. Names of the contractor, supervisor, mason and mate who gave their opinion are not published for the interest of research.

Rarely he gets time to visit the construction site. According to Duggar workers of Banjara caste are most efficient and are hard working group. Second best are the workers from Kherwara Tehsil of Udaipur district. He prefers to appoint more women labourers as he noticed that those are much more efficient than the men. He paid money for the work and to get the work alone is his concern. He cannot tell about the health of labourers, their family condition, social status and economy. He could only tell that women workers are more sincere to their assigned work than the men. But if sometimes he has to tell something to the labourers, he always tells the men who understand him easily.

Contractor 2. He also likes to appoint more women labourers than men as labourers. They are sincere, hard working and have no courage to ignore the contractor or the supervisors. He noticed that the men try to make groups. They keep/acquire some knowledge on rules of labour law where as women are ignorant.

Sometimes these male labourers try to organise all the labourers of both the sexes and to place proposals of their demands which is never possible for women labourers alone. He also told that this work is not suited to women's health and women are also exploited even sexually by men at construction site. Men take advantage of their ignorance.

Contractor 3. Construction work is not suited to women. Previously he did not recruit any women as a labourer in his work but that hampered his work. The masons and other male labourers did not like to work in his site and called it as a desert without any women. They joined in nearby working sites where there are women labourers. He appointed women; some of these are beautiful and attractive and gradually he noticed his men workers returned to his construction site.

According to the contractor, construction work as earning source is a recent phenomenon for this place. When he started his work at the Zawar Mines he faced labour problem. He himself went to each and every neighbouring villages. That time these villagers had land on which they depended throughout the year. They were least interested/ bothered to earn cash money, which also came from their corps. With the development and progress of the mines, many cultivators lost their land against some compensation. They lost their primary source of income; compensation was nothing in comparison to their losses. They ultimately faced economic crisis. Gradually they decided to work in construction. With the influence of industrialization they began to give more importance to their dresses, ornaments and other luxury items; then they brought their women with them to work in construction who are much preferred by the contractors. Finally contractors gave more importance to women labourers than men. Now construction labour is much more related to women than to men.

(B) Petty Contractor (of Brick Masonry)

He prefers to keep women labourers upon whom he may show his power more than in case of men. Male labourers never work beyond their limited assignment and hours. They are more careful of their wages, payment and agreements. They have the tendency to oppose their superior workers. They never listen to orders especially from the masons with whom they always have a rival attitude. They do not like to carry the *'tagari'* on head which they think is only meant for women. All the time they quarrel among themselves. The women are never like that. They obey everybody, even the male labourers of same rank. They do not argue with contractor or with mason. Carrying of *'tagari'* on head is not regarded as a degraded job by them and they believe it is natural.

(C) Supervisor

The adivasi women labourers are not at all well behaved. They do not know how to behave. They give preference to hunger and sex (just like non-human creatures) which breaks their morality. It is very difficult to guide them to work in a proper way. Throughout the working hours he has to keep strict watch on them. If he becomes a little sympathetic or shows a little kindness to them, they take the advantage and "try to seat on his head". He is not in favour of women to work whether it is a construction site or even in Government office. He thinks that women are meant to be housewives and they may work in field. He was against of keeping women to work at their construction work. According to Adhir these women tell lies, misuse the money and sometimes run away with men; for which Adhir has to face consequences. He wants to make best use of his women labourers, atleast for half an hour more than prescribed and that satisfied him. These "junglees" are fool, cannot "see the time" so it is easy to take more works from them.

(D) Contractor-Cum Labour Supervisor

Women are more efficient and sincere workers than men; so they are preferred. Moreover the women keep the construction site look charming; nobody feels tired. Some of the women are really charming. He likes to be close to them, but they are not regarded as "cultured". Their food habits, dress, way of life differ very much from the "standard" way of life. They are strong like beasts, they know how to attract men. They wear *Kabjo* (short blouse) to attract the opposite sex instead of *Polka*.

(E) Mason

These women are poor, come to work as per economic need. They are illiterate, without having any knowledge of rules which prompts the contractors to cheat them. He never hesitates to talk freely or to be very close to these women both sexually and mentally. He said that these women are not intelligent, scared of loosing the job.

A few inhabitants of villages Padla, and Ratakhet were interviewed regarding their opinion on the women construction workers. The findings are summarised here.

(F) Villagers

1. ***Sunni Kharari, Female, 55 years***

According to Sunni Kharari (a Bhil woman of Padla village, age approximately 55 years) construction work is not liked by her. Many parents send their daughters to work at the construction site to earn money for the family as it is one of the easiest way of earning, but it brings many difficulties to the family and society. The women who go to work at construction site think themselves free from the restrictions of their society. They develop friendship with many people by whom these women are exploited. They come from the site after the day's work late, and make on excuse of overtime work. Their parents also give them indulgence telling them nothing and they quarrel with the villagers if the villagers say anything suspecting their daughters' character. According to Sunni, "it is better to die of starvation than to send daughters on wrong path".

2. ***Amro Kharari, Male, 65 years***

He lives in village Padla, told that construction work in an easy source of income, but it is bringing disharmony in their Bhil society. The women construction labourers lose their character easily. So it is better not to send the women to construction work.

3. ***Lilabati Harmer, Female, 35 years***

The women construction labourers mix up with many men outside their community for extra income. As these women earn cash money from their job, they get taste of money, they grow greedy to earn more utilising their sexual ability. These construction labourers try to have more freedom which brings sorrow in their life; which breaks many families and brings quarrels, hampers in the peaceful life of the society. She does not mix up with these women, who do not behave well and encash their sexual ability. Sometimes her husband is attracted towards some of the construction labourers which disturbs her. These women come out of the village; try to adopt the new fashions; wear dresses and ornaments like town people and look smart which attracts men. She does not like this type of attitude and behaviour. If any of the women construction labourer visits her, she does not entertain the woman joyfully. She gets suspicious. During religious festivals, ceremonies all the villagers gather but these women construction labourers are not entertained like the other women who are totally housewives and work in the fields. She feels scared if her daughter talks to any women construction labourer of her (daughter's) own age.

Sometimes the villagers tell the women to stop working in construction and they reply quickly, "you give us food, clothes, then we shall not go". According to her from other sources the income may be less than from the construction work. Yet those are better. The women construction labourers become rude, quarrelsome, and cunning. They lose their simplicity, health and grow old early.

4. *Punam Hurdamari, Male, 45 years*

He is Lilabati's husband, working at Zawar Mines. He supported Lilabati. But he has some sympathy for the women construction labourers. He said,"they are neglected in our society". Generally the young generation is connected with construction work who sometimes do not know what is not accepted by the society. They can be tempted easily by others at the construction site. Due to their simplicity, they are easily cheated by the workers.

5. *Punam Kharari, Male, 50 years*

He lives in village Dharicha of Udaipur district told that generally those who have no or negligible amount of land send their women to work in construction. They may also send their women for mud filling and other works. Which the women do not agree to do as they have to work with their village men. They give many excuses that they are cheated by co-workers through whom they get work. But, they are equally well cheated by the contractors and several other persons every day at the construction site. They may earn a little more amount from construction work but there they have to work harder than in other works. Some of the women even ignore to work in field which is too boaring for them. He concluded that specially the women of young generation do not like to work under the villagers' eyes. They try to be free, go far away to work where they could enjoy themselves, which ultimately brings sorrow in their lives. He never allows her family members to make friends with these women. The construction labourers are never entertained by them. Generally they keep minimum interaction with them.

Beside these, opinion from the women labourers were recorded on their position in their own society and at construction site. All of these are more or less similar. One of these is given below :—

Lali Bai (38 years) of Ratakhet village of Udaipur is attached with construction work for atleast seven years. She told that generally due to economic need they are forced to come and join the construction work. Their society, their villagers do not want to send their daughters, wives and sisters to work in the construction site but they are helpless and rather are forced by economic pressure to send them to work in the construction site. Even then they advise them to work at any other unskilled sector instead of construction work. According to Lali and other women there is no other work which is equally convenient for them as the construction work. It is well remunerative, they get advantage to take loan without interest from the construction site. Beside these they can make friendship with others outside their village. They can exchange their views with those persons of both the sexes by which they can learn more and more of the world.

In their villages the villagers specially those who never send their women to work at the construction site suspect them, there is jealousy mixed with hate from their side on the construction work. Jealousy is noticed maximum among the non-working women. If a construction worker wears new dresses, they think that those are presented by somebody else with whom she runs an illegal relationship. They avoid to talk freely with these women. Even they are treated in this manner by those villagers they are always in a helpful attitude to them. These villagers do not feel shy to take loan from them in their urgency.

It is not possible for these construction workers to attend all the social function due to their engagement in work and when they attend those after hectic labour they generally like to get some enjoyment from the side of society. So they always try to avoid to listen the gossips against them which make them sorry. It is true that there are several women having illegal relationship with men at the site but all are not the same.

It is seen that in the construction site women labourers are regarded as simple, sincere and hard working. The contractors have less interaction with these women, but the supervisors, the mates and masons have direct contact with them and in general they appreciate these women for their sincerity in work and are regarded as much better than the male labourers.

On the other hand in their villages they are not so much appreciated. It is true that they are sent to work to the construction site by their family members but the family members do not prefer this work. They are rather forced to send their daughters, wives and sisters due to economic need. They always are suspicious on those women that they are doing wrong.

6

Position of Bhil Women in their Society

Ethnography of the tribe helps people to get some knowledge on the position of their women in their society.

The women in their society are as a whole regarded as inferior to their men in each and every sphere of their life. When a son borns in a Bhil family everybody gets happy because a son is responsible to maintain the lineage. So in case of a male child, the *dai* (mid wife) gets five rupees, some vegetables, some cereals and a set of new cloth while for a female child a *dai* gets only two and quarter rupees with vegetables and cereals as a charge for her services. When a male child borns the *dai* beats a plate (*thali*) but when a female child borns she beats a winnowing fan. Beating of winnowing fan symbolizes to do work and beating of *thali* symbolizes to eat food. In this way from the very childhood differentiation between male and female starts. The birth of a daughter gives her father a source of income in form of her labour and also in form of bride price. Whereas, in case of a male child, in his marrige his father has to pay bride price. Even then a son is more preferred to keep the family tree continuous.

Generally a Bhil woman works more than a man. Before marriage she works for her father's or brother's family and after marriage for her husband's family.

During field investigation it is observed that the Bhil parents are not so eager to educate their daughters. They say that a daughter is meant for another family so what is the use to educate them. They never will go for white collar job. So it is useless to educate a daughter. Instead during the time of education they can give some economic support to the family by her services at any unskilled sector.

When a girl reaches her marriageable age, her parents wait till someone approaches to them for her hand. The bride price customarily is not so high but gradually it is increasing. Now-a-days they claim it both in cash and kind. The girl's parents wait till a party offers them a satisfactory amount as bride price. Bride price is regarded as compensation for the future loss of their daughter's service is paid to her deprived parents. It varies from rupees three hundred to five hundred beside the articles paid in kind. After marriage when the couple reaches the bridegroom's house, they are taken to a place where some cowdung and a hoe are kept. The new husband picks up the hoe and throws it away. Then his wife follows the hoe and brings it back and keeps it at its right place. This is repeated for three or five or seven times. It signifies that a man may do anything according to his wishes but a woman should work is such a systematic way which is beneficial for the family. It is the responsibility of a woman to keep the family peaceful and she should work systematically.

A newly married couple enters a room where two pitchers are already placed. The bride takes the pitchers and goes to the nearby well or stream to fetch water. On her return she has to stand by the side of the door. The husband pays her rupee one and twenty-five paisa and takes the pitcher from her. It signifies that the man will feed her in lieu of her services.

In a Bhil family in general man is the head of family and holds the authority. A woman may officiate as family head in absence of any aged or grown-up male member.

Divorce is frequent among them. Both the parties have right to divorce. In case of a man the reasons for divorce are barrenness, quarrels between husband and wife, insanity and extra marital relationship. A man can divorce even for his wife's unduly long stay with her parents or being reluctant to stay with him or due to her laziness and suspicious behaviour.

A woman can divorce her husband if he is cruel or if she cannot adjust with her co-wives, or when she falls in love with a person, other than her husband, whom she wants to marry.

The rules of divorce are more helpful to men than women. Generally women are not permitted to divorce until the bride price is refunded in part or full. A man has nothing to pay to his wife as compensation. When a man intends to divorce his wife who does not want divorce from her husband, the husband tortures her. Then automatically the wife calls her relatives. The husband entertains them with food and drink and in their presence he tears a small piece from one corner of his turban and ties it to a corner of the wife's sari with a token amount telling her that from that moment she would not longer be his wife. Many times when the husband is so eager to divorce his wife for his own interest, not for her fault, he does not claim the bride price in return. She is allowed to go for widow marriage or *natra*. A man at a time may keep several wives but a woman is not allowed to do so. Even extra-marital relationship for a woman is highly objectionable. If a separated woman stays with her parents and after sometimes the husband like to take her back her parents may ask for a compensation.

In the Bhil society an unmarried woman gets considerable freedom of movement. She can talk, laugh, mix up freely with a man of their own society. Pre-marital relationship is also tolerated till a woman gets pregnant. When an unmarried girl gets pregnant it becomes difficult for her parents to get a match for her. In such a case the man responsible for pregnancy becomes free after paying some compensation to the girls parents.

A woman generally has no right to officiate at any ritual. She is considered as impure, her participation in some rituals and ceremonies are even tabooed. The ritual impurity is defined on the basis of their menses and delivery.

In case of their traditional panchayat it is seen that posts of such a panchayat is always occupied by the Bhil men. Women are never allowed to hold a post. They are only permitted to attend the meetings.

From the above discussion it can be said that.women in the Bhil society enjoy a subordinate status to their men. The women construction labourers inspite of being a lucrative economic source could not be able to ameliorate their status in their society.

7

Conclusion

The previous chapters dealt with the women labourers associated with construction work. The study has been done in the Udaipur city, in its industrial belt and also in the mining area of Udaipur district of Rajasthan among the Bhil women.

In this study it is found that women workers are mostly drawn from economically lower strata of rural society which comprises mostly of the landless agricultural labourers or the cultivators having less productive and non-irrigated land; majority of them come from the nuclear type of families. These casual daily wage earners, who work in the unorganized sectors, take this employment to supplement their family income. They suffer sporadic and seasonal employment as such, are mostly under employed.

In this study the author tried to see the emergent way of life of those tribal women who work as unskilled labour in construction site. The study has mainly two divisions (a) It dealt with the women workers in the construction site, reasons which force them to work as wage earners in construction site, how and when they become attached with construction work (b) Women at their home. This part dealt with their families, kins, villagers. Their attitude towards these women and the position of these women are studied.

With the spread of industrialization, these women began to join to work in construction industry. They are forced to seek employment in the modern sector to increase the meagre family earning but gave rise to many abuses and exploitations.

In all the studied construction site it is found that these women always occupy the lowest position in the work structure. They are unskilled labourers and even after doing heavy work, they get their wage less than all other workers.

It is noticed that the women construction labourers come to be attached with construction work at their very early age. They even start to work before completion of their 12 years of age. As per plantation Labour Act No. 69 of 1951 'no child who has not completed his/her 12th year shall be allowed to work in any plantation.'

At the construction site the women labourers mainly work as the assistants. Beside these works they also water the newly built structure, they do mud filling and also do the work of *reti chhankna* (extraction of stone etc. from sand). Sometimes they carry the heavy stone slabs, cement bags from one place to another. All these works are heavy for women. Women are sometimes asked to do the work of belder. They prepare concrete mixture which is the work of belder but they do not get the wage of belder for doing the work of belder.

They have a fixed working hours. They have to work eight hours daily with half an hour lunch break. It is found that everyday they have to work at least half an hour more for which they get no extra money. The contractors keep them busy throughout the day. They are cheated by the contractors and the mediators who never tell them the exact time. They even cannot take their food and take some rest with peace. The supervisors begin to drive them sometimes even after fifteen minutes of lunch break. Generally they are not given more than twenty minutes of lunch hour. The contractors and the supervisors say that they deduct ten minutes from lunch break to assemble the women labourers to restart the work. Otherwise they can not start the work at the actual time. Loss of a minute is a great loss of work to the contractors. But it is observed in all the cases, these women have to work atleast half an hour more everyday for which they get no overtime benefit. These women are treated as inhuman being in their working place. The wage of a woman construction labourer is Rs. 5/- per day. It is found in many places that the women are paid less. In the same construction site differentiation in wage is marked. Their wages are paid on weekly basis or fortnightly or on monthly basis. Those who are paid on monthly basis get their payment on the seventh day of the month. They get holidays on Holi, Depawali, Independence Day, etc.

It is already mentioned that in general women come to be attached with construction work at their very early age. They even continue to work till their age around 50 years but it completely depends on their health condition. The contractor, their supervisors, etc. never like to appoint the women above 40 years (approximately) of age. They prefer to engage young and healthy women in such a manual labour. It is found that maximum number of women belong to the age up to 35 years of age.

These women initially become attached with construction work through the persons one generation above or with some elderly members of same generation. After that they usually come with friends or with the persons of same generation.

The studied women construction workers are divided into two divisions the local and the migrant labourers. The migrant labourers take temporary shelter at or very close to the construction site. In the Reliance Chemotex construction site these migrant labourers are accommodated in the rented huts close to the construction site. These huts are not suitable for habitation. They live there in a subhuman state. Their huts are devoid of proper ventilation, sanitation, cooking or bathing place and also drinking water facility. In the Zawar Mines the labourers are accommodated in the newly constructed buildings which are not finished. These buildings are really half constructed. There is no facility of electricity, no tap water is available. They are not allowed to use the toilet of those buildings. In this situation in a room many women are accommodated which creates space problem also.

In the Reliance Chemotex construction site, during working hours the workers get the opportunity to drink comparatively clean water but those who live in the temporary shelter get no such advantage. They take water collected from nearby well. In Zawar Mines they take water from nearby water connection taken by the employer for their work. They are not given any sanitory facility. In the site of Reliance Chemotex construction work the women go at a distant place, at a culvert where they carry water with them. They urinate here and there even in the construction site. In Zawar Mines they use jungle as their toilet and urinate here and there even inside the newly constructed buildings. Their working and living condition is not satisfactory. The contractors, supervisors, masons even the labourers exploit them (discussed in previous chapters). These unskilled labourers do not get previledges to acquire skill which require time, effort and money. Parents do not think of or take care even bother about providing education and training to them, employers also do not invest for their training which is thought to be a loss for those employers. As a result they have been disproportionately bunched in the low-paid inferior occupation.

These women are not given any medical facilities except any major accident during the work at site. They have to do hardwork throughout the long working hours. Due to heavy load of work, and specially due to carrying of heavy stone slab, cement bags, and bowls full with concrete mixture female diseases are very common among them. They feel headache, stomache and pains all over the body. They get tired, with sickly appearance, get old so quickly. Then they are terminated from the job or not selected as a labourer to work in the site. They get no pension benefit. For their sickness and weak health they cannot perform the household duties or cannot earn for the family and as a result they become the burden to the family and ultimately to the society. There is no creche home for their children. Many women bring their small children with them when they come to work. They keep their children at the working site, uncared and unattended. The contractors and the supervisors do not like them to attend their breast feeding babies. Sometimes the children get hungry, they start crying but the women are not allowed to attend those. In this situation sometimes the women are forced to tell lie. Such a woman in that condition tells that she has to go to toilet and instead of going latrine she attends the child. But the supervisors always keep their eyes on each and every woman. They immediately drive the women from that place to join the work. They even sometimes give no permission to those women who wants to go to toilet.

There is a canteen in the Reliance Chemotex construction site from where all the workers can take food. It is found that the women generally do not take food from there. They bring their lunch packet with them. They can not afford to take food from there. It is costly to them. They very occasionally take tea from there. Sometimes their male friends (those who have) offer them tea and snacks from the canteen. In the site of Zawar Mines there is no such canteen.

These women labourers enjoy lower status than the non-tribal women labourers and the male labourers. It is observed that they are burdened with the major share of work. These women are shy, always afraid of losing the job, suffer from inferiority complex. This is an advantage to the contractors and the supervisors to make them burdened with hardwork. They are very low paid workers and have a very low status. They even have no courage to oppose against injustice.

The women in their (Bhil) community are lower in position than their men. They get no priviledge as an earner in the family. On the other hand their family members take it as a very common and usual phenomena. They are sometimes not allowed to spend a single coin of their earning as per their wishes. They have to hide a part of their earning from their guardians and keep it for their own use. Construction work could not help them to elevate their position in the society. In addition they are even suspected, abused and exploited by their family, village and ultimately by their society members. They are neither treated with prestige in the construction site nor in their society.

So atleast to improve their position at the construction site, there should be some amenities for those women labourers. There should be better regulations of condition of casual labourer. Decasualization scheme should be explored to ensure greater security of employment for casual workers.

Radha Kamal Mukherjee has suggested that where work is continued for atleast two years, definite rules should be formed compelling contractors to provide proper housing and sanitory arrangements, treatment of cases of sickness including accommodation for infections diseases and accidents (Sengupta, 1960). It is a very good proposal in favour of these labourers. At least for the migrant labourers there should be housing, sanitory and drinking water facilities.

The construction labourers should have their employment card. The contractors and the supervisors should strictly follow the rules regarding their wages and working hours. There should be drinking water facility and proper sanitory system and atleast for the migrant labourers there should be housing, sanitory, drinking water facilities at their temporary settlement and the shopping facilities should be provided them. There should be provision of maternity leave benefit, family planning incentives, creches, and educational facilities for the children of all the workers. It would help the construction work to become more attractive and women labourers could make their families benefited more, which ultimately would help those to improve their status in their society.

Appendix 1

Case Studies

Case 1

Rupli Kharari

Rupli Kharari, a Bhil woman, is a construction worker for last seven years. She lives in village Ratakhet of Udaipur district with her husband. She works at Reliance construction site.

She could not give birth to a child and that is the root of all her troubles. Her husband is very much unhappy and considered her responsible for bad luck and unhappiness to their family. Beside her husband all her husband's kin-folk have the same attitude and no one has any sympathy for her. She visited many sacred places nearby and made offerings; went to the village medicine man, who gave her medicinesbut she could not conceive. She herself is eager to have a child may it be a male or female, though male child is preferred in their society; but even a female child is better than none. She went to hospital; the doctor checked her thoroughly; she was under treatment for months and spent a lot on medicines and travelling. At last doctor found that a minor operation is needed to cure her for which she has to spent minimum rupees two hundred and fifty only as the cost of midicines. They have already taken some loan from Baniya to maintain the family. She has to meet the debt. Her husband does not pay any money to meet the repayment. He is also not so eager to pay her for the operation.

Her husband (Khomaji) is also a construction worker and works as a mason (*Kharigar*) in Udaipur. He is in love with a married Bhil woman labourer. He neglectes Rupli Bai and often tells her that he would bring a second wife someday. She hopes that if she could get a child he will change his mind. She could ask her husband for money or take loan from Baniya, but there is no certainty that she will get a child. If she would get a child, she hopes her husband will meet the loan. But if not, then he will not pay a single coin. It is quite impossible for her to meet all the loans of Baniya. She is an irregular construction labourer because of her poor health condition. She has menstrual trouble which made her unable to do such type of heavy work. She is so weak and looks pale.

Her husband earns ten rupees per day, but he stopped paying any money to Rupli. Instead, he teases her of her barrenness. One day she told him that after the operation she may get a child; her husband replied that he has least interest. He has lost all hopes, and he does not like to pay for operation. He again threatens her that he would bring another woman and divorce her on account of her childlessness. Since then she is frightened of divorce. "If he will divorce me then where shall I go? If I go "natra" then my husband may claim the amount he spent on our marriage. Nobody is interested to pay such an amount for a barren woman who is at the edge of her youth". She has lost her parents. Her brothers and sisters are busy and happy with their own families. She can go and stay with them for a few days but she does not wish to stay long with them and make them unhappy. She always prays to god for a child and hopes that her husband may reconsider her case.

Rupli is attached with construction work for seven years, and for the first time she was taken by her husband's cousin sister to work as construction labourer. Before marriage she never worked as a construction labourer. Her parents are cultivators. Her in-laws were also cultivators. Her husband did not like to work in the fields and he sold to Bahiya his share of land about one bigha to built their new hut with the amount. After marriage for first three years he cared well for her. Gradually he became unhappy due to her barrenness. His relatives and friends always reminded him of her weakness. He started to neglect her. This situation forced her to work at construction site, though it does not suit her because she is not quite strong to do a hard labour.

At construction site she has to attend and do several types of work as carrying heavy loads of cement, lime, morter or bricks on head, helping to built the *Vara* (temporary wooden platform), bringing water, sweeping the floor, cleaning implements, bringing tea to her mason.

During working hours she becomes tired. She cannot tell anybody to listen her trouble and to give her some rest. Right from contractor to the mason, everybody is so irritated if she takes rest for a while.

At construction site Lali, Barju, Mangni are her husband's elder sisters and Damri, Bhamri, Narayani are her husband's cousins' wives. Dulki is her husband's cousin's son's wife. Rupli (another girl of same name), Bulki and Basanti are her husband's cousins' daughters. All of her sisters-in-law are older than her. She maintains a distance with them and always she feels uneasy in their presence. She has to talk with them politely. In turn they keep a strict vigilance on Rupli. She is not even allowed to talk to her friends about her husband's attitude and behaviour towards her.

Among all her sisters-in-law, Narayani Baî pays least attention to her, because she is busy with her own affairs. She is proud for her youth and beauty to attract others to her. Narayani is not liked by the women of the group. She is guilty so she has no courage to blame others. Rupli does not like to talk to Narayani who has love and extramarital sex with another man who has wife and children. Rupli can easily relate the case with her own husband's case. So she cannot bear Narayani. Bulki, Dulki, Basanti, Rupli are so sweet with her and she is also very much affectionate to them. Those three are helpful to Rupli when she is tired. During lunch break manytimes it is observed that those children help her by cleaning her utensils and bringing water for her.

Rupli's friends are sweet to her. In absence of her relatives she talks to them freely about her problems. One day during lunch hour she was talking with Tejki Bai about her own problems. Tejki also is a sufferer with an identical problem. She told Rupli that somebody saw her (Rupli's) husband roaming in the city with a woman, whom he saw another day at the same construction site where Khomaji works. These two women planned that one day they would go to that construction site to meet that woman and would try to dissude her and the affair. Similarly Rupli will help Tejki to solve Tejki's problems. While they were discussing Lali came there, they stopped their discussion and changed the topic. Khomaji is Lali's brother. So Lali does not like outsider's interference in Rupli's matters. Lali has sympathies for Rupli as she is a little different type of woman Sometimes Lali tries to solve their quarrels but she is able to solve the problems only temporarily.

Rupli's lunch generally includes a piece of *roti* and *mirchi*. She is trying to save money for the operation.

She is hesitant and shy to talk to men at the construction site. Her husband had asked others at the site to keep a vigil on her. If she commits a mistake her husband gets scope to blame her and may divorce her. She is very much afraid of divorce. She loves Khomaji, and can never think of another woman in her place. Now-a-days he spends most of his nights outside. She is unhappy. She cannot tell about the details of his absence. If she asks him this question, he replies "I do not feel happy to spend nights with you. It is better to spend with other women". Rupli always tries to make him happy by cooking items which he likes most, bringing *daru* for him. Everyday she waits for him till mid night sometimes she weeps; sometimes she dreams that all the problems will be solved by birth of her child after she has gone for an operation.

Her husband asked her to go back to her parental village. He has already taken all of her ornaments, which were given by him at the time of their marriage. She has nothing upon which she can depend. Her health does not permit her to work at construction site for long. If he drives her out, "how she will manage to spend her life". One of her friends told her that the man will not drive her out as he also have some weakness for her; if he wanted to do so he should not have waited for seven years. She can please him by giving birth to a child.

Rupli works under petty contractor of brick masonry under the head contractor. She feels so uneasy and shy to work in their presence. She is also afraid of them as they scold her all the time on even minor issue. If any time the petty contractor named Allauddin gets angry, she does not feel so nervous as she knows Lali will tackle him and make him cool by frightening him of stopping of work of the whole group. Lali always points out his weak points and faults. Then Allauddin feels unhappy and tries to recover from it by blaming the head contractor. Sometimes women understand that Allauddin plays tricks with them. They become so angry and Lali waits for a good chance to give him a lesson. According to Rupli, Allauddin though gives pressure to them to work more and more but he is not so inhuman. He knows how to please the women. Once Allauddin conceded the request of women labourers and allowed them to go to cinema and gave them two rupees to each labourer. On other occasion he gave one rupee to two women whose lunch was eaten by dogs.

She never worked as migrant labourers. As she is married woman, it is not possible for her to work as migrant labourer. Nobody will look it positively. Rupli has a fear that in her absence her husband may bring in another woman, whom he brings in and entertains while he goes to her brothers house for two/three days. For this reason and due to her illness she does not go to work as migrant labourer.

She earns about rupees one hundred in a month as she is an irregular worker. She spends at best sixty rupees and repays the debt saving ten to fifteen rupees per month.

When she is sick and unable to work she spends from her savings.

When she is without any job at construction site, she goes to jungle, collects wood and sells to the market.

According to Rupli in their Bhil society construction work is not preferred, though maximum number of women work at construction site.

Case 2

Barju Bai

Barju Bai is a widow of nearly forty five years age, lives in village Ratakhat of Girwa Tehsil. She has two daughters and two sons, daughters are married. Her husband died seven years ago when their youngest son was only two years old. They then lived in village Deuli from where she was forced to return back to her parental village with her children as her brother-in-law cheated her by occupying all their land. Her sons are now 10 and 9 years old respectively. They do not perform any work to give economic support to the family. Barju does not like to engage them at construction site to earn in their this early age.

Barju's husband was a landowner and cultivator, who had five bighas of land. They had never worked in construction before his death. Barju never wish to attach her sons to construction work. She wishes to send them, specially the youngest to school.

At first she was attached with the job through Lali Bai--who is her younger sister. At first she did not like to do such heavy work, but gradually she could make herself adjusted with the work and atmosphere. She could arrange for her daughter's marriage after starting the work at construction site.

At the site she talks only to Damuri, who is with a moral character. She does not talk uselessly, specially with men.

She never brought her daughters to work at construction site. Barju prefers agricultural work to construction work. She feels proud that she could arrange her daughters' marriages to cultivators' families. She is happy that her daughters are leading happy married life.

In the time without any construction work at hand she faces economic difficulties. During that period she goes to jungle collects *muli* (wood), sells those to earn some money and to maintain the family, but the earning is not sufficient and they starve. She takes loan from relatives. But the relatives are not in position to give her loan.

She never works as migrant labour. She has children and her widow mother. Her mother lives with them in the village, it is not possible for her to go to work and stay in other village. Her mother takes food from Bhamri (Barju's sister-in-law). The old woman used to hide some food from her share for Barju's sons. One day it was noticed by Bhamri. She then quarrelled with Barju and her mother. Next day Bhamri did not give any food to her mother-in-law and Lali (Barju's sister) fed her. For a few days Chandni got no food from Bhamri. Narayani fed her for a few days as Chandni used to look after her child during her absence. In due course Bhamri again changed her attitude, reconciled and fed Chandi Bai, her mother-in-law. Lali, Bhamri, and other relatives blamed Barju for this happening because it was for her sons and Chandni had to suffer. Barju saves money. She cooks once a day. Every evening her sons get Government food. During evening sometimes she does not cook and take the food if there is any food left by her sons after taking lunch. She does so to save money to repay the loan. She knows that the Government food is insufficient hence Chandni (her mother) gives them some food from her own share. After the quarrel with Bhamri, Chandni takes meal once in a day from Bhamri and another meal from Lali.

Barju has to work a lot. Early morning she gets up, does all the household works including cleaning, washing, cooking etc. then takes a *roti* with tea and offers some breakfast to her sons and keeps the rest of the food for her sons. She takes her lunch packet of roti with chillies, jaggery or onion and rarely with cooked vegetables with her and leaves for the construction site within 7 a.m.

After finishing the day's work at construction site, when Barju returns home, she can see her sons either busy to play or to take food from Government officials come by jeep. But sometimes if she becomes late, they go to sleep.

During long absence from home she remembers her sons. Sometimes Lali used to scold the children as they do nothing, even do not think for their mother, Lali orders them to clean utensils or bring water which Barju never likes. Sometimes she quarrels with Lali for that.

According to Barju, the girls who work at construction sites their parents face difficulties at the time of the arrangement of their marriage. Sometimes the husbands become so suspicious on the wives which brings quarrel in a girl's marital life.

She said "construction labourers are not treated as human creatures by the contractors". During working hours we have to work constantly without any stop. They feel so tired, feel pain throughout the body. Barju feels giddy due to the work from morning till dusk by collection of cement mixture, going to mason, supplying the materials to him again coming to collect the materials. During summer they feel terrible. Once a woman of about 30 years of age became faint due to heat. But contractors did not bother. According to her they are not given clean filtered drinking water. They have no security of employment, or their health.

They are not given the minimum standard of working and living conditions.

Sweat comes across their faces, they become tired but cannot stop work even for a moment to brush off their hair or to clean the sweat. They wait till lunch time. During lunch time they feel hungry and tired. They just swallow the food and drink water, clean utensils and immediately go to sleep. But it is just for a few minutes. The contractor again calls them to re-start the work. Though her legs do not want to work, whole body pains so badly, yet she has to join work after lunch hour for the attraction of day's wage.

Case 3

Narayani Bai

Narayani is attached to construction work from her childhood when she was about 10 years of age and was brought by her mother who herself was a construction labourer. Her father was also a labourer though they had some non-irrigated land which they used to cultivate during rainy season. She was married to labourer's family, who has only a land where they can grow vegetables. Her parents-in-law and her husband are also construction labourer. After her marriage Narayani is again brought to construction work, this time by her husband's cousin sister-Lali Bai. She has a 3 (three) years old child. They are only three members living together. Her husband works at a different construction site. Her mother-in-law lives in a separate hut with her youngest son who is also a labourer at construction site where Narayani works. Her mother-in-law grows vegetables in the small piece of land for family use. Her husband does not claim but her mother-in-law sends to them their share.

She likes to work at construction site because in other works she finds no charm and in construction work she has an extra income. In construction work she may earn beside five rupees, two rupees per day as extra money by exploiting her sex. She may spend those to buy *Kulpi, polka, tamaccu, daru,* clips, ribbons etc. The money she gets from a man who is attached with the same construction work. He is a driller with whom she is in love.

As Narayani is attractive and good looking, with friendly behaviours. People at construction site try to be close or intimate with her. She gets preference from men at the site. Their contractor gives her to works like 'reti chhankna' or works at ground floor. According to him Narayani is fat, so it is not easy for her work upstairs. But in case of other women he ignores these.

She has no objection to talk to men working at the same construction site when they work together with men, they have to work together. So why she should not be friendly with them—she cannot understand it. They may be friendly and according to her "they may even love each other". It is not a fault or crime for a woman. Friendliness is necessary for better progress of work. At the site her affair with the man is only encouraged by Lali not by others. The other women of the village work at the same site try to avoid Narayani and they tell the other villagers about Narayani's activities at the construction site.

Narayani said that majority of the men are migrant labourers came to work leaving their own villages. They feel tired, sometimes frustated. So they try to get other woman for their enjoyment both mental and physical. The women get extra money, presentations and priviledges at work. She gets several such proposals from even petty contractors, supervisors, masons, labourers. She is always ready to accept the proposals. She is ready to give them company during day time, but not at night. At night she has to stay at home. Otherwise all the villagers would come to know that she is really exploiting her sex which is not permitted for a married woman in Bhil society. Her husband never allows her to work as migrant labourer. She is not permitted to stay outside at night even in her parents' house.

According to Narayani if a man likes to make sexual relationship with a woman, he asks for some food or tea or tabacco from the woman. Always asking for food drink and tobacco does not signify an offer of sex relationship. Manytimes due to very friendly behaviour (though it is rare) also they ask those from each others. But when it is meant the sex relation there is some other cognitive behaviour and approaches. If she agrees it, it signifies that she has accepted the man's proposal for sex relation. There are many girls at construction sites with same type of relationship with men in the construction site.

In her case that man never said that he wishes to marry her. His family resides in Ajmer. In Udaipur he migrated to work where he got intimacy with Narayani. Narayani also loves him, likes to continue the relationship with him but she does not want to marry him. If the man would marry her, then she has to leave her son. It is not possible for her.

She never talks to the contractor. But she is so friendly with her petty contractor, who tries to understand their difficulties and tries to solved the problems.

After finishing work at a construction site, she stays at home and takes rest for a few days, she works at home, goes to the jungle to collect wood (fuel) and sells those. She also collects fuel for her own use. Sometimes she goes to see films and to meet her relatives. At that time she has to depend totally on her husband's earnings sometimes they take some loan from the Baniya.

When she comes to work, keeps her son with Lali's mother. Narayani sometimes gives her lunch for this job.

She does not like to stay at home idle. She likes to earn money and prefers construction work to which she is habituated from her childhood. Moreover they need money. Her husband has no objection to send her for construction work. After getting her wage, she gives the amount to her husband keeping five to ten rupees for her. She likes to deposit some of her earnings with Baniya to buy ornaments.

At home she has to work alone. Only during her menstruation her husband brings water, cooks the meals.

At construction site she is known as a talkative woman. The old women of their group do not appreciate her. She is avoided and to an extent hated by them. They do not talk to her.

Since her husband came to know about her illegal relationship with a man working in the same construction site she said "there is misunderstanding between her and her husband". He came to know from his younger brother and other women labourers working with Narayani in the same construction site. Her husband wants her to work with him in his present working site. She refused it. Narayani said. "If I work along with my husband, nobody will talk to me. I will be always in my husband's vigil. I will not get any importance for the contractor, supervisor etc. and other workers. Moreover I will not be able to meet with the man". Then her husband tried to stop her to work at construction site. During February, 1979 she paid not even a single coin of her earning. Then her husband become to angry. He tried to stop her work forcefully. She denied to pay the money, as her husband kept all her ornaments with Baniya. She told him that she may pay him if he would bring the ornaments from Baniya. She wished to get back all her ornaments as there was a wedding in the village. She wished to wear it. But due to economic difficulties her husband was not able to give her assurance that when he will bring ornaments. Due to this reason she denied to pay even a single coin.

One day her husband told her that she should go to work to the same site otherwise she would not be permitted to stay at his home. She felt unhappy. She disobeyed him. Throughout the day she was disturbed. She consulted Lali how to solve the problems. At the time of returning home Lali and Narayani went to liquor shop, bought one bottle of liquor, then went to Lali's hut. Lali prepared onion *pakora* (onion fried with spices) invited Narayani's husband (Lali's cousin). She offered both of them *daru* and onion *pakora*, made them happy and forgetting everything the man brought her with him to home. Throughout the evening Lali tried to convince him that his wife is not bad. All the stories about her are not true. He agreed to Lali to send Narayani to work with her. But after a few days, one day after returning home again he began to quarrel. Next day she could not come to work at construction site, went to her parents, told everything to them (hiding her relation with the man). They at first told her to leave construction work and to do what her husband wants or likes. She denied to do so. Then they told her to work in their field, from where she may earn rupees six per day atleast by selling vegetables. Even they told to stay with them. None of the ideas was thought suitable by her. She requested her father to solve the problem. Following day after returning from construction site she saw her father was busy to make his son-in-law understand everything, and to solve the problem. He (her father) told him to bring back all of the ornaments and to give Narayani permission to work at the same construction site. Narayani's husband kept himself quite. When his father-in-law left, Narayani was beaten heavily by him. So ultimately she stopped the work. Sometimes she thinks to leave him. But she cannot think to leave her son. Her husband after few days brought all her ornaments from Baniya taking a loan of rupees three hundred from his contractor to please her. She paid him rupees one hundred and twenty five only (which she refused to pay earlier). But after a few days when she found her husband in a happy mood, went to work without his permission. When he (her husband) came to know felt unhappy. She met with the man told him all the happenings. Actually Narayani does not like to leave her husband and son for the man but on the other hand it is also impossible for her to cut off all relations with the man at the construction site.

One day the man fell down from 30 feet height while he was at work, he was injured and admitted into hospital. Narayani came to know this through Lali. She went to hospital to see him. When the man was discharged from hospital again met with Narayani at the road, near Railway crossing. Both of them were so happy, began to gossip forgetting everything. Other women and also her brother-in-law noticed them complained to her husband who again beat her so badly. From next day she got fever, admitted to hospital. After returning from hospital did not join in construction work as she is five months pregnant. Everybody tells that she is carrying the man's child.

Case 4

Nani Damor

Nani Damor lives with her parents. She was married to an employee in a Mill at Ahmedabad with whom she spent her days happily. But after few months of their marriage he died. After his death, she lived with her parents-in-law, received an offer of marriage after one year from her brother-in-law whom she did not like but she was treated as family property as her husband paid bride price during their marriage. So she could not deny and married her husband's younger brother. After that she gave birth to her daughter within a year. She found that her husband was not interested in her. He was in love with another girl of aneighbouringvillage. One day he brought his second wife. He began to neglect Nani. One day she approached them to allow her to go to her parents along with her daughter. They allowed her. After three/four months her unmarried sister-in-law came to take away the child. She also told Nani that in case Nani wishes to marry again, they will claim rupees two hundred and fifty only which they paid to her parents at the time of marriage. She refused to leave her daughter but the girl after many quarrels forcefully had taken the baby and Nani was left without her only child. Nani was unhappy, wept for a long. She had no right on the child. She could not do anything. By this time the family began to feel her as burden specially her "Bhabi"(brother's wife). Who was very much annoyed with her. Nani felt that she should not stay without her own earnings. She talked to her friends, some of whom are labourers. After taking permission from her parents she came and joined to work in construction site. After a month and few days her elder brother's daughter also came with her and joined construction work. She is attached to construction work under the same contractor from two years. She works here as a migrant labourer.

She supplies concrete mixture to the mason, gets rupees fiveper day. She is quite, does not talk to others. Her mason is from Kumawat caste who is friendly with her. He is kind and considerate. Though their income depends on the swiftness of their helpers, yet he never tells Nani to work fast. When she feels tired, the mason gives her chance of a little rest. Many of the mason earn as much as rupees twenty per day. But this man does not like to treat his helper so pressurize with heavy work load.

The present building under construction is second work in her life. The first one was built before this building under the same contractor. When they finished the building the contractor got the contract of this building. Hence she was not without a job. They heard this contractor has many other works in hand which will continue for several years. She cannot think herself without job. In that case she will be again a burden on the family which she does not like to be.

In her parents' family, nobody has any objection to send her in construction. They only ask her not to run away with another man. Then even do notbotherso much if she mixes up freely with men but society will not accept her if she gets pregnant.

She is able to earn rupees one hundred and forty only per month. She sends rupees fifty to her parents in the village from where she came to work at the construction site. Rest rupees sixty she keeps with her as her expenditure, mainly to buy cereals, vegetable, oil etc. and a meagre amount, not more than rupees thirty as saving she keeps for her off-periods (when there will be no job).

This way, once she saved rupees eighty six after working for three months. She bought new clothes and some luxury items for herself and for her daughter. Then went to the village where her parents-in-law live to visit her daughter where her elder sister also lives. The child often comes to her hut, plays with other children. Nani wanted to see her. So Nani's sister brought her. She gave all the articles to her daughter. When Nani's husband's family came to know of this they returned back everything. Nani then came back with a very disturbed and unhappy mind.

She was unhappy, her father felt pity for her, went to her in-laws, prayed to take the child with them. Then through Gaon Panchayet she could get the child in a condition that when the girl will be grown up, Nani will send her back to her own village. (But at that time if the girl will deny to go to her father, then the case will be different). By that time if Nani will go on *Natra* then she will be forced to send back the child. This is one of the reason for which Nani does not like to marry again. She pays to her parents as the expense of her child. She wants to keep her daughter with her but as construction site is not the safe place, many accidents take place in construction site, she never brought her child. Every month she visits the child at home.

She likes to save money for her and her child's future. She has no interest to buy clothes. She has three sets of clothes in which only one is good. Others are dirty these two she wears at the construction site. The clean and good set she wears when visits her village, relatives and friends.

When she stays at home, she does all the work. Her two brothers live together with their wives and children. The youngest sister-in-law is sympathetic to Nani who helps her at home.

Previously she was outspoken, but now she is not the same. Only she quarrels with her elder sister-in-law who irritates her specially when she was without job.

Nani told that the villagers do not like the unfortunate women like Nani. They blame her that she killed her husband, burnt the second family, gave birth to an unfortunate child, came to disturb another family. They neglect Nani and also other women, who are unfortunate like her.

They also tell stories that women like Nani definitely are in love and have affairs at construction site. According to her generally married women never come to work as construction labour unless they are poor, needy and unfortunate like her.

Case 5

Bhamri Bai

Bhamri Bai (35 years approx.) comes to work to the Reliance Chemotex construction site from the village Ratakhet of Girwa tehsil of Udaipur. She has two daughters. She has to do the works at home and also at the construction site. Her daughters help her in household duties by bringing water, sweeping the floor but cooking and lion's share of household work is done by her.

Generally her husband does not prefer her to engage in construction work but they have less fertile non irrigated land where they cannot produce a quantity of food to run the family even for three months. He himself also does labour in construction sites. Sometimes he gets agricultural labour which he prefers most. He does not like the construction work rather is forced due to economic constraints sometimes to do the job and to send Bhamri to work in construction site.

Bhamri said that before her marriage she never worked in construction site. Her father is economically well off. He has land close to a water source so it is not difficult for him to irrigate the land. After marriage at the beginning she had not to come to work in the construction site but with the increase in family they feeled that she should earn money for betterment of the family. At first she came to work with her husband's elder brother's wife.

In the construction site she works from 8 a.m. or 8.30 a.m. till lunch break at about 1.10 p.m. One of her friends at the site brings water for her also. They take food together. After finishing the lunch she cleans the utensils, cleans her teeth with a silver needer called "Khota" and gossips with friends and then sometimes she begins to sleep. She can sleep at the most ten to fifteen minutes. The work continues upto 5.30 p.m. and sometimes even 5.45 p.m. She cannot see watch. She can know the time by asking her mason and other labourers. After finishing the day's work at the construction site she returns home with other members of the group and after reaching home she cleans the utensils, goes to the nearby well to wash hands and feet and to bring water. She prepares tea, roti and sabjji, distribute those to all the family members and then take roti and sabjji and goes to bed.

Generally her daughters do not cook but occasionally they, specially the younger daughter cooks the night's sabjji.

At the construction site she has to work hard. She sometimes feels so tired. When she feels so tired, she takes one or two days leave (without payment). During those days she goes to the nearby jungle to collect firewood for household use.

Case 6

Gopi Bai

Gopi Bai (48 years approx.) comes to work from the village names Kanpur of Girwa tehsil of Udaipur district. She does not like to work with non-tribal women because according to her the non-tribal women are very quarrelsome and reluctant in duties. The non-tribal women always look down upon them. There may be some exceptions but she cannot tell even a single name.

Gopi Bai has to objection to work in construction site. She says "If we do not work then who will feed us? construction work is the best avenue to earn cash.

She works as a local worker. She never is allowed to work as migrant labourer. She has three children, the daughter who is her eldest child comes to work with her in the construction site.

She says that she prefers her daughter to work with her or very close to her. She keeps her vigil on the girl. She says that her daughter is also so gentle. She never talks useless and mixes up so freely with the workers in the same construction site. Nobody in the construction site and in the village can tell any unpleasant talk about the girl.

Case 7

Dulki Bai

Dulki Bai is only 20 years (approx.) old married girl works throughout the day with her tired face. Sweat comes across her chicks. She wipes it again and again and work throughout the day with all her sincerity. She was ill and was admitted in hospital and is discharged twenty days ago. In her family there are only two members her husband Thikalal and herself. Before six or seven months she gave birth of a male child who died just after delivery. She is not able to tell the exact cause of the child's death but feels sorry for it. From the time of her delivery she remains so sick. She has a menstrual cycle and due to heavy non stop bleeding she was admitted to hospital. She looks pale, her hands are so thin, a bony structure just covered with skin. But she is so pretty with fair skin colour and a beautiful, attractive face.

Dulki Bai became a construction labourer after her marriage because her husband's earning is not sufficient to maintain a family. He does agricultural labour in a Baniya's field, works throughout the year and gets only Rs.100/- per month.

Dulki lost her parents in her childhood. She stayed with her two married sisters families alternately. Her sisters families have land. They work in the field. She also used to work with them in their field. Her sisters were very much anxious to arrange for her marriage. Thikalal is her second sister's husband's distant relative. Thikalal is not so rich, but according to Dulki he is a nice fellow. His parents are old, stay in the same village near their hut who spend their livelihood by doing labour in others' field. Sometimes Thikalal gives some monetory support to them. Dulki sometimes instead of working in the construction site work in others field also, but most of the time she works as construction work as agricultural labour is not available easily. She is attached with construction work by her husband's cousin sister Lali.

She prefers to work in construction site because she can earn more money than the other jobs. Such a laborious job is not suited for her, even then she prefers to work in construction site for better earning. After finishing a construction work, she sits at home for a few days and again gets involved in another construction work. During those days she goes to jungle to cut wood and sell in the market.

At the construction site she has to work more than eight hours. She gets Rs. 5/- per day as her wage.

Lali, Narayani, Bhamri, Bardi, Mangni, Damri all are related to her. Narayani, Damri, and Bhamri are her *Jethanis* (husband's elder brother's wifes). She does not like the matter of Narayani's extra marital relationship with a man, but she never likes to gossip with others discussing the matter. It is completely Narayani's personal matter. Dulki cannot tell anything to Narayani against her affair because Narayani is helpful to her and manytimes helps her by sharing her jobs such as to fill up the *tagari* with concrete mixture. Manytimes she gives her loan. One day during lunch hour, Narayani was taking bath in the site in an open place near the water tank. The water tank is situated at a corner of the construction site. She called Dulki, gave her all personal belongings such as ornaments, *Polka*, bra and chunri to Dulki. It was a very unpleasant scene. Dulki was feeling so uneasy. At first Narayani made her body and hair wet. Then she rubbed some sand thoroughly on her hair and began to rub her hands and legs with sand. Then she rubbed her head, hands and legs with a piece of stone adding a little water. After that at last she has taken bath. Here sand and stone are used as soap. All the women became so angry with Narayani's such activities. They said that Narayani should not take bath in such a place. But Dulki told that they do not get time to take bath daily. They only get time to wash their hands and feet. Sometimes they even take bath after a week. So they become so dirty. Their body smells, it stincts. So sometimes she also feels to get a bath but she feels shy to take bath at the construction site. Dulki also told that Narayani should not take bath in the construction site.

Case 8

Samsu Ahiri

Samsu Ahiri (18 years approx.) is attached with construction work from her childhood (about 12 years of her age). She at first came to work with her father. She sometimes also work as labourer in road construction work.

Her father is mainly a cultivator, having two bighas of non-irrigated land. Sometimes he works in Mahajan's field as share cropper, where he gets half share of the production. But it is very difficult to get a job in a mahajan's field. So sometimes when he gets no job he comes to work at construction site as construction labourer. Her mother never works outside home except in field. She sometimes brings firewood from jungle for family use when she goes for cattle rearing.

Samsu is attached with the present construction site through her friends. She works here as migrant labourer came to work after Holi and continued to work till the rainy season. During rainy season she returned to her village and became busy in their own field. During that time there was proposal of her marriage from a village named Banna. But this time the crop is less. They even have no sufficient food. So Samsu's father has taken one year more time to marry his daughter. If Samsu is married just now then the family will loss her income and the family will starve. Due to such reason Samsu again come to work at the construction site. The bridegroom's side do not know that Samsu works in construction site. She works hiding it from them.

In the construction site she stays with her village friends. She stays in a room with six other women. It is her temporary shelter. Early in the morning she leaves her bed washes hands and feet. She keeps her bed rolled at a corner then sweeps the floor. She collects water from a nearby water source. It may be a direct connection from water tank or from a nearby pond. She keeps water for drinking and cooking purpose. Then she prepares tea and distributes it to every body and after that helps in cooking. She prepares her roti separately and sabjji collectively with others.

During lunch hour she takes bath if she gets any time. If there is no time, she washes her hands and feet and then take her lunch. After finishing the lunch, she cleans her utensils and if possible her clothes. She washes her clothes at the time of taking bath or after taking lunch. After that again joins the work. After finishing the days work, sometimes she goes to the market to buy vegetables and returns the temporary shelter where she again cooks food, chat with friends take the food and go to sleep. In this way she passes her days in the construction site.

She generally visits her village once in a month after getting her payment from the construction site. She pays her earning to her father keeping atleast Rs. 20/- with her for her personal expenditure in the construction site. Her Monday's payment she spends to buy vegetables and her other daily needed commodities. She brings *ata* (wheat flour) from her own village. (In this site Monday is declared as holiday and when they work on the holiday, payment is made on the spot on that day).

Once her father got his great toe injured at the time of making boundary at their own household. At that time Samsu had to take loan of Rs. 50/- from her contractor. It is adjusted with her payment.

Samsu does not like to work in construction site. She cannot work so much. Everyday she feels pains in hands, leg, head and feels so tired. But she must work otherwise her family would starve. She thinks that how her father will run his family after her marriage.

Her would be husband is an agricultural labourer and can read and write. She does not like an agricultural labourer to be her husband. She dreams of a husband who has a big share of land and where there is plenty of food.

Case 9

Ganga Bai

Ganga Bai (21years approx.) has come to work with her father from the village named Bilak. They are migrant labourers. In their village they have no land and their parents used to work as agricultural labourers in others' field but their income was not sufficient to maintain a five membered (husband, wife and three children) family. Due to this reason one day her father talked with some of his friends for some better earnings and they suggested him to work as construction labourer. As per their advise or suggestion her father made contact with some construction labourers of their village and with their help he joined the construction work. Gradually he brought Ganga, his eldest child to work in the construction site. Ganga's mother is unable to join construction work because she has to look after the other children.

In the Reliance Chemotex construction site Ganga and her father are working since three months. They have taken their temporary shelter very close to the construction site. Both of them work as labourers. Ganga and her father generally visit their village once in a month. Sometimes Ganga visits the village to meet her mother and brother and sister. She goes with some other persons of the village when her father remain busy with construction work. Generally they halt not more than three days in their village. At the time of return from village to the construction site they take their *ata* (flour) for the next month.

They take roti and sabjji twice daily. Vegetables are purchased from the local market. Ganga has to do all the works like cooking, bringing water, sweeping, cleaning and washing. She has to complete the day's cooking before coming to work at the construction site and just after finishing the work she returns to the temporary shelter and becomes busy again in cooking. Her father helps her by bringing vegetables from market and sometimes by bringing water when he feels that his daughter is really so tired with the day's work.

Each of them get Rs. 5/- per day as their wage. Payment is done on monthly basis. She always pays her total earnings to her father. He gives her Rs. 2/- or Rs. 3/- as her hand expenses. Her father pays her some extra money to purchase ribbon, clip, bindi etc.

Generally her father pays some money to her mother for family maintenance. Some amount is spent to buy clothes. An amount is paid to baniya from whom they have taken loan. They hardly can save any money from their earning.

According to Ganga Bai, in the present site the contractors and supervisors in the construction site give preference to the local labourers. She cannot tell the exact reason of this. It may be due to their expertisation in work or as they are older group working with contractor for long time.

Case 10

Nagri Bai

Nagri Bai (20 years approx.) is a local worker works in the construction site at Zawar Mines. She lives in Padla village. She is attached with construction work since three years. She is attached with construction work by her friends and now also came to work with her friends.

Her father works in Zawar Mines. He does not like to send Nagri to work in the construction site. But Nagri is forced to work as construction labourer because they have need of money. It is true that her father's earning is enough to maintain the family but her father drink so much and he spends his most of the income in drinks. She has three brothers and one sister. Her sister is youngest of all. She stays at home, helps her mother in household duties, her two elder brothers are married and have their separate families. The eldest brother lives in Ahmedabad. Her younger brother's earning is not sufficient to maintain the family. Due to economic need she is forced to come and join the construction work.

Nagri is a beautiful girl, full with youth. She is so attractive. Manytimes Nagri is asked by some males, specially the *Karigars* (masons)for her company. In lieu of that they pay Nagri some money. Unfortunately before seven months Nagri became pregnant. Her parents asked her who is the person responsible for it. She denied to say a single word. Her parents tried to identify the man but failed to identify him. Upto three months of her pregnancy she worked in the construction site, hiding it from her parents and all the construction workers. After three months she told it to some of her friends. The supervisor also came to know about her pregnancy. He stopped her to work in the construction site. Then during fourth month the issue was aborted. During abortion her life was in danger so her parents shifted her in Udaipur hospital. Her father kept all her and her mother's *jewar* (ornaments) with the Baniya and brought money for her treatment. After that she had to take rest for two months and then again she has joined the construction work. They faced troubles from the village. They had to arrange for a community feast to get excused from the villagers angers, abuses and threatenings.

Presently they have no *jewar*, no savings. This time she is so tired unable to do hard manual labour but for her livelihood, to maintain family she is forced to come and join construction work. Her father does not talk with her. He till now cannot tolerate her. Her mother repeatedly tells her not to do such type of mistakes. Generally she reaches home late. If her mother asks her she simply says due to overtime work she became so late. The other girls of the village avoid her due to her such type of behaviour. They only keep some formal relationship with her.

Case 11

Shanti Bai

Shanti Bai is a girl of only 15 years (approx.) of age. She is attached with construction work from about her 12 years of age. She at first came to work with her cousin Kamli, and from that time she is attached with construction work under the same contractor. She comes to work with her cousin Kamla from the village Padla of Girwa tehsil of Udaipur district.

In their family she is the only earning member. Her father has two bighas of non-irrigated land at present where there is only grass, which is used as fodder for their cattles including only two goats and a cow. Her father works in field, and when there is no work in field, generally stay ideal at home. He does not like to work in construction site and not allows his wife to work in construction site who only performs the household duties along with cattle herding. Shanti has three younger brothers among whom two read in school and the youngest is so small, performs no work only except playing. She has an elder sister who at her eight years of age was taken by their maternal uncle with him to work at his home. As their maternal uncle has no daughter and as his wife with a poor health he faces great trouble with the household work. His sons read in school so there is nobody for cattle herding. So he asked Shanti's father to take their eldest child with him. Shanti's father agreed with the proposal. It is also helpful for him because of his poor economic condition.

Shanti informed that in their society in general males are happier, they get preference in all the spheres of their lives. In their family, her brothers are given advantage to read and to go to school. She also wishes to read but her parents tell that it is useless to educate her. A girl is meant for another family and she will never go to earn as teacher or to work in office. On the other hand it is better for a girl to help her mother in household duties or to earn some money by doing some unskilled job. Her elder sister has gone with her maternal uncle to help her family by doing household work and by cattle herding. His sonsalso read in school. There in their maternal uncle's house she earns her bread by working whole day and Shanti earns her bread by doing construction work. Shanti also has to assist her mother in her household work also. During holidays she goes for cattle herding.

When she gets her payment, she pays it to her father. Only she can keep two rupees from her Monday's income. At Zawar Mines Monday's income is paid on that day at the spot after the day's work is finished. Her parents know that on monday she gets only Rs. 3/-. Her father buys all the food, cloth by her earning. The money is not sufficient to maintain the family. Only they can get *roti* (one or two at a time) of maize twice daily. Sometimes they take it with *sak* (vegetables). She has only two *ghaghras*, two *kabjos* and two *udnis*. One set of dress she uses at home and the another is worn by her when she comes to work at construction site.

Weekly she can keep Rs. 2/- which she spends in *churi*, *seu* (apple)etc. Her father brought one pair of shoe for her during winter.

Her parents always tell her not to mix up freely with the males. She is always told by them, "dant mat nikalo" (don't show your teeth that means don't lough in the construction site) but she is so friendly with the workers of both the sexes specially of their village. All the males treat her as a small girl, like their younger sister but their supervisor is not at all a considerate man. He always tries to get more and more job from them. Once he beats her. She began to cry loudly. During that time contractor was present there who scold the supervisor.

Shanti says that they have to do hard labour in the construction site. She comes everday with her cousin who is senior to her. After completion of day's work she returns home with her cousin.

Appendix 2
Bibliography

Agarwal, B.C. and Kumkum Rai March, 1980 *Women, Television and Rural Development study of SITE in a Rajasthan village.* Ahmedabad : Space Application Centre.

Banerjee, Sukumar 1978 "Tribal Women in Coal Field Area", in *Tribal Women in India,* edited by Indian Anthropological Society, Calcutta: Indian Anthropological society.

Bhasin, K. 1972 *The position of Women in India.* Bombay.

Chowdhury, N.C. 1978 *"Womenhood in Tribal India".* Calcutta : Indian Anthropological Society.

Dandiya, C.K. 1975 *Women in Rajasthan* Jaipur : Rajasthan University.

Dasgupta, Pranab Kumar 1978 "Tribal women in industrial context" in *Tribal Women in India* edited by Indian Anthropological Society; Calcutta : Indian Anthropological Society.

Doshi, J.K. n.d. *Social Structure and Cultural Change in a Bhil Village*, Delhi : New Heights.

Government of Rajasthan January, 1980 *Rajasthan Raj Patra Extraordinary, Part IV (Guha). Sub-Section-II.*

Guha Thakurta, S.N. 1980 *Contract Labour in Construction Industry, Calcutta* : Firma KLM Pvt. Ltd.

Hate, C.A. 1969. *Changing Status of Women in Modern India*, Delhi : Vikas Publication.

Herskovits, M.J. 1974 Economic Anthropology, New Delhi : Eurasia Publishing House Pvt. Ltd.

Indian Council for Social Science Research 1975 *Status of Women in India* A synopsis of the report of the National Commission Calcutta : Allied Publishers.

Kapur, P. 1970 *Marriage and the working women in India.* Delhi : Vikas Publication.

Kapur, P. 1972 "Women in the Home", *The Position of Women in India*, ed. K. Bhasin, Bombay.

Mann, R.S. 1980 *Hakkipikki*, Trapers and Sellers Calcutta: Anthropological Servey of India.

Mishra, A.D. 1994 *Problems and Prospects of Working Women in Urban India*, New Delhi : Mittal Publication.

Rani, K. 1976 *Role Conflict in Working Women. Chetna* Publishers.

Russel, R.V. and R.B. Hiralal 1975 *Tribes and Castes of the Central Provinces of India.* Vol. II, Delhi. Cosmo Publication.

Sahay Prasad, Sushama 1988 *Tribal Women Labourers* (Aspects of Economic and Physical Exploitation) Delhi : Gyan Publishing House.

Saran, A.B., A.N. Sandhwar, 1990 *Problems of Women Workers in Unorganized Sectors* New Delhi : Northern Book Centre.

Sen, J. 1978 "Status of women among Tribes", *Tribal Women in India*, Indian Anthropological Society, Calcutta.

Sengupta, P. 1960 *Women Workers of India*. Bombay : Asia Publishing House.

Shashi 1978 *The Tribal Women of India*, Delhi.

Sherring, M.A. 1975 *The Tribes and Castes of Rajasthan*, Delhi : Cosmo Publication.

Sinha, G.P., S.N. Ranade 1975 *Women Construction Workers*. Indian Council for Social Science Research. Bombay : Allied Publishers.

Srinivas, M.N. 1978 *Changing Position of Women in India*. New Delhi : Oxford University Press.

Swaminathan, M.S. "A Fair Deal for Migrant Labour", *Souvenir, of South Asia Regional Symposium of International Association of Human Biology, National Symposium of Child with Handicap.*

7th Annual conference of Indian Society of Human genetics. Department of Zoology, Ranchi University, Ranchi.

Vyas, N.N. and Chowdhury, 1970 *The Frontier Bhil and Meghwals*. Udaipur: Tribal Research Institute.

INDEX

Age at which women join the construction site, 31
Age group of women labourers, 31
Ahiri, Samsu, 125
Allauddin, 108
Attachment with the construction work through Kins/Non-Kins, 33
Ata, 58, 128

Bahinji, 64
Bai, Barju, 109
Bai, Bhamri, 55, 77, 121
Bai, Dulki, 106, 123
Bai, Ganga, 128
Bai, Gopi, 122
Bai, Lila, 89
Bai, Lali, 112
Bai, Nagri, 129
Bai, Narayani, 54, 106
Bai, Shanti, 131
Bai, Tulsi, 74
Baniya, 104
Banjara, 19, 84
Basanti, 106
Beldar, 26, 50
Bhabi, 118
Bhanra, 49
Bhil family, 94
Bhil society, 38, 95
Bhils of Udaipur, 19
Bhil woman, 93
Bilak village, 46
Bindi, 60
Brahman, 17
Brick & stone masonry, 18
Bulki, 106

Chandni, 110
Chhori, 64
Chowdhury construction, 21, 23, 25
Churi, 132
Construction of Staff Quarters under Hindustan Zinc Ltd., 20
Construction on mill, 13
Contractor-cum-Labour Supervisor, 86
Coolie, 22, 26

Dai, 92
Damor, Nani, 117
Dangi, 21
dant mat nikalo, 132
Daru, 107
Depawali, 98
Dhankabara village, 45
Discrimination with tribals, 67

Discussion with women labourers, 68
Duggar workers, 84
Dungarpur, 44
Economic condition, 69
Economic constraints, 70

Family type of the Informant, 32
First coming in the construction site with the person, 33

Gaon Panchayet, 120
Ghaghras, 132
Girwa Tehsil, 109

Hali, 98
Hardamari, Punam, 88
Harmer, Lilabati, 87
Holidays as per Labour law, 48

Independence Day, 98

Jain of Ajmer, 19
Jewar, 130
Jhagda, 63
Jhilani Bros, 22
Jhupri, 46
Jogandars, 49
Junglees, 86

Kabja, 57, 86
Kalal caste, 21
Kankroli Village, 44
Karigars, 130
Kajal, 60
Kharari, Amro, 87
Kharari, Punam, 89
Kharari, Rupli, 103
Kharari, Sunni, 87
Kherwara, 26
Khomaji, 107
Kind of Constractors, 83
K.K. Construction, 21
K.K. Construction site, 45
Kumawat Contractor, 24

Labour Act No. 69 of 1951, 97
Lake Palace, Udaipur, 19
Lohar, 21

Makki, 80
Marital status of labourer, 32
Mason, 86
Mataji, 64
Mavli, 26
Mirchi, 107
Mukherjee, Radha Kamal, 102
Muli, 110

Nathdwara, 26
Natra, 120
Non-tribal labourers, 62

Pakora, 116
Panch Patel, 44
Pani pilana, 58
Petty Contractor, 85
Plantation Labour Act No. 69 of 1951, 30
Polka, 58, 86

Rajasthan—a dry place, 38
Rajput of Jaipur, 19
Rana Pratap Nagar, 15
Ratakhet of Udaipur, 103
Reinforcement Cement Concrete (R.C.C.), 22
Reliance chemotex construction site, 43, 53
Reliance Chemotex Textile Industries, Udaipur, 14, 16

Reti Chhankna, 50, 58, 61
Roti, 58, 107
Rupli, 106

Sak, 132
Sabjji, 58
Sunni Contractor, 19
Sunni Muslim Contractor, 24
Supervisor, 85

Tagari, 49, 71
Tamaccu, 113
Tejki's problems, 106
Thali, 92
Three categories of labourers, 18
Tokri, 56
"Try to seat on his head," 86

Unskilled women, 71
Urake le aye, 63

Vara, 105

Who brought the women to present construction work, 33
Women as a grown up unmarried daughter, 73
  as a working wife, 76
  as a daughter-in-law, 78
  as a mother-in-law, 79
  as a working widow, 80
  as a divorced woman, 81
Women comming with Kins / Non-Kins, 34
Women construction workers, 30
Women labourers, 62
Women's agreement with contractor, 49
Wood collection from jungle, 40

Zawar Mines, 15, 34, 35
Zawar Mines, Udaipur, 15, 34, 35, 48, 99